# Acknowledgm

As I sit down to write these acknowledgments for my second book, I'm reminded of the journey that led me here. The path has been full of learning, growth, and, of course, support from some truly remarkable people.

First and foremost, to my family—thank you for always standing by me, providing endless encouragement, and believing in me even when I doubted myself. Your love and patience have been my greatest source of strength, and I'm forever grateful to have you by my side.

To my clients, past and present: this book wouldn't exist without your trust and the lessons I've learned from your unique journeys. Though the case studies here are fictionalized to protect your privacy, the heart of each story is based on your real experiences. You inspire me daily, and I'm honoured to continue helping you navigate the world of finance.

A heartfelt thanks to my father, and team members. Your feedback and invaluable insights have shaped my approach and inspired me to keep pushing myself. You've helped me improve not only as a writer but as a financial planner and communicator.

Writing my first book was a huge milestone, but this second one has brought its own set of challenges, excitement, and joy. To everyone who read and supported the first book, your encouragement has motivated me to continue sharing my knowledge. I hope this book resonates with you just as much as the first one did—and if you're new to my work, I'm thrilled to have you along for the ride.

Finally, to my readers: thank you for picking up this book. Your curiosity, eagerness to learn, and commitment to taking charge of your financial future are what make this journey so worthwhile. I hope this book provides you with valuable insights and sparks meaningful conversations as you continue to learn and grow.

Here's to another step in this incredible journey—together!

# FOREWORD

Welcome to a journey unlike any other—a rollercoaster ride through the world of wealth, wisdom, and some truly eye-opening money truths! If you've ever felt like managing your finances is as complicated as solving a Rubik's cube blindfolded, trust me, you're not alone. This book isn't here to preach or drown you in financial jargon. Nope, we're here to make the complex simple, the boring exciting, and the intimidating downright approachable.

Let's face it—most of us spend more time scrolling social media than understanding our own money. We invest (or don't) based on hearsay, gut feelings, or that one uncle who claims he knows the market better than Warren Buffett. And diversification? It sounds like a fancy word only financial gurus throw around, right? Well, this book is here to tell you otherwise.

In these pages, you'll meet people just like you—individuals who've wrestled with questions like, "Am I doing enough?" and "What if something goes wrong?" You'll get to see how the power of planning, the magic of compounding, and the wisdom of diversification can transform anyone—from landlords to salaried employees—into confident wealth builders.

And don't worry, it's not all serious! This book is full of relatable stories, practical advice, and even a few laughs along the way. We'll break down financial concepts in a way that makes sense, so you can finally take charge of your money—and your future.

So, grab a cup of coffee (or tea, if you're fancy), settle into your favorite chair, and get ready to uncover the secrets to building wealth, protecting your future, and securing your peace of mind.

Here's to understanding money, building dreams, and finding hope—one smart decision at a time.

Let's dive in!

## Disclaimers

I know, I know! Disclaimers aren't usually the most exciting way to start a book, and you're probably wondering why I'm beginning with this. But bear with me—read these first, and I promise you'll appreciate them as you dive into the chapters. They'll help you understand and enjoy the book much more. So, let's get through them together before we move on!

## Disclaimer 1:

Before you continue, I want you to know that this book is not your typical financial textbook. You won't find theory-heavy explanations on SIPs, SWPs, STPs, or the differences between large-cap and small-cap funds. There will be brief mentions of these terms, but they won't be the focus here. Think of this more as a storybook that features real-life-inspired case studies, each with practical insights that you can apply in your own financial journey.

## Disclaimer 2:

As mentioned earlier, This book is written like a story, and while the case studies may seem real, they are fictional. Inspired by real experiences, names and details have been adjusted for privacy. These scenarios reflect practical situations but shouldn't be applied exactly—always consult a financial expert for your own decisions.

## Disclaimer 3:

In most of the case studies, you'll find suggestions centered on Indian mutual funds. I have strong faith in mutual funds as a wealth-building tool, so they feature prominently throughout the book. And to avoid repetition and make things smoother, here's the all-important disclaimer that applies to every chapter:

"Mutual fund investments are subject to market risks. Please read the scheme-related documents carefully before investing. Past performance does not guarantee future returns."

These disclaimers apply to all chapters, so you can continue reading with full understanding of the context. Let's get started!

## About the Author

**Vishal Muralidharan** is a **Certified Financial Planner, Chartered Retirement Advisor**, and an **AMFI-Registered Mutual Fund Distributor** with a strong legacy in the financial industry. His father, **Mr. Ganesan Muralidharan**, is also a seasoned mutual fund distributor who founded **GSM Investment Services** in 2003. Growing up in a finance-focused environment, Vishal developed a deep passion for wealth management and investment planning.

In 2019, he officially joined **GSM Investment Services**, carrying forward the firm's 23-year legacy of trust and expertise. He has also authored the book **"Retire Early Through Mutual Funds,"** which is available on **Amazon** and **Flipkart**. Through his writing, Vishal simplifies financial concepts with engaging storytelling, real-world insights, and practical strategies to help readers take control of their financial future.

Beyond finance, Vishal enjoys exploring new ideas, engaging in thought-provoking discussions, and sharing insights that help people make informed financial decisions.

## Hi, I'm Ganesh Sharma—your fictional financial planner!

The author of this book thought, 'Why go on this journey alone when I can create someone to guide you?' So here I am, your companion through the world of finance! I'll be walking you through all the stories, case studies, and lessons in this book, offering insights and advice along the way. Think of me as the certified financial planner for all the cases we're about to explore.

But let's be clear—I'm not a real person, just a character created by the author to make your reading experience more engaging and fun. So, as you read, consider me your financial GPS, helping you navigate through the concepts, but the real journey is yours to take!

# Why Goal-Based Financial Planning is Your Best Friend

Imagine your finances as a road trip. Without a destination, you might end up driving in circles, burning fuel, and getting nowhere. But with a clear goal—be it reaching the mountains, exploring the beach, or visiting grandma—you know exactly which route to take, how much fuel you need, and where to make pit stops. That's exactly what goal-based financial planning does for your money: it gives you direction, purpose, and clarity.

## Setting the Stage with Relatable Stories

Let's start with two characters: Ravi and Priya.

- Ravi saves whatever is left at the end of the month, which is often nothing. He's worried but tells himself, *"I'll start saving seriously next year."*

- Priya, on the other hand, has a plan. She wants to buy her own house in 10 years, so she invests a fixed amount every month for her down payment.

Fast forward a decade: Priya is sipping chai in her new balcony, while Ravi is still wondering where all his salary went. Priya's story is not about earning more but about knowing what she wanted and planning for it.

## Why Planning with Goals Feels Less Like Math and More Like Life

If budgeting and saving sound like boring math, it's because we think of them in isolation. But when you tie them to your dreams—a world tour, your kids' education, or retiring early—it suddenly becomes exciting. Think of it this way:

- Every ₹5,000 you save could be a step closer to your dream vacation.

- Each SIP you invest could fund your child's MBA.

- That emergency fund could mean sleeping peacefully even when life throws curveballs.

Goal-based planning isn't about restricting your spending; it's about enabling your dreams. Instead of asking, *"How much should I save?"* you start asking, *"What am I saving for?"* It shifts the focus from sacrifice to purpose.

This book is here to show you that financial planning doesn't have to be overwhelming or tedious. Through case studies, we'll explore how everyday people turned their financial messes into success stories—all by setting clear goals and sticking to them. By the end, you'll realize that financial planning isn't just about money; it's about living your best life.

Ready to dive in? Let's get started!

## Your Financial Fact: The Rule of 72

Want to know how long it'll take for your money to double? Here's a fun little trick to figure it out: the **Rule of 72**!

Here's how it works:

**72 ÷ Interest Rate = Years to Double Your Money**

Let's say you invest ₹1,00,000 at an annual return of 9%. Using the Rule of 72, you can figure out how long it will take for your ₹1,00,000 to grow to ₹2,00,000:

**72 ÷ 9 = 8 years**. That's right—your ₹1,00,000 doubles in 8 years with a 9% return.

Now, here's your mission:

1. Pick an interest rate—maybe you're getting 10%, 12%, or 15% return on your investments.

2. Plug the numbers into the Rule of 72. How long will it take for your ₹1,00,000 to turn into ₹2,00,000?

**Important Note**:

This rule is a helpful estimate, but it's not guaranteed. The actual returns you get can vary depending on market conditions, risk, and other factors. So, while the Rule of 72 is a great tool to visualize growth, remember that real-world results might differ.

**Bonus Challenge**:

Tell a friend about the Rule of 72 and see if they know it! They'll be impressed by your money magic skills. ✴

# Case Study 1

## The Wedding Budget That Didn't Break the Bank

Weddings in India are a big deal—where every family member, neighbour, and long-lost relative must show up. For Meera and Arjun, their wedding wasn't just about getting married but also avoiding a financial mess: full of different costs, unexpected expenses, and a lot of pressure to get everything right. This is the story of how they planned a wedding that was not only beautiful but also financially smart—without having to sell a kidney!

## The Problem: Big Dreams, Bigger Bills

It all started in March 2019. Meera and Arjun were over the moon about their engagement. Their families? Even more excited. But soon, excitement turned into Excel sheets, and their wedding budget resembled a Bollywood movie budget: ₹50 lakhs!

- **Venue:** ₹12 lakhs (*"But it's AC, with chandeliers!"*)

- **Catering:** ₹15 lakhs (*"Beta, it's only ₹1,500 per plate for paneer tikka!"*)

- **Photography:** ₹5 lakhs (*"Everyone must look like movie stars!"*)

- **Decor:** ₹8 lakhs (*"It has to feel like a Director Shankar set!"*)

When Arjun jokingly asked if they should start crowdfunding, Meera replied, *"Or maybe we should run away and have a Zoom wedding instead."*

## The Realization: Keep It Simple, Keep It Real

One thing was clear to Meera and Arjun—they didn't want to take on debt or make their parents spend all their savings for a one-day event. But Meera's father sighed, saying, "If I had planned and saved earlier, I would have given you a grand wedding."

Meera laughed and replied, *"Appa, adhukunu time travel panna mudiyuma? (is it possible to travel back in time?) It's okay. It's not necessary for parents to put all their money into a wedding. We'll handle it."*

That conversation sparked an idea for the couple. They decided to take their time and plan the wedding a year later. *"It's a win-win,"* Meera joked. *"We get to roam around cafés and corner seats in theaters without wedding stress for a whole year. And we'll save up for our dream wedding too!"*

**The Game Plan: Saving Smart, Not Hard**

Once the decision to postpone the wedding was made, Meera and Arjun sat down with a notebook, a calculator, and two steaming cups of filter coffee to figure out their finances. After hours of crunching numbers and debates, they came to a solid conclusion.

With their combined salaries and disciplined budgeting, they could save ₹5,00,000 over the next year. Adding this to the ₹10,00,000 they already had in their respective savings accounts, they were set on a budget within ₹15,00,000 for the wedding.

The couple was set on their goal of sticking to ₹15,00,000.

After finalizing their ₹15,00,000 target, Arjun leaned back and said, "Okay, with this ₹10,00,000 in savings, we'll need to add ₹40,000 every month to reach our goal. That'll get us to approximately ₹15,00,000."

Meera raised an eyebrow, "Wow, Arjun, when did you become a finance expert?"

"Thank you, thank you," Arjun said with a mock bow. "But seriously, we need to find a better way to grow this money. A savings account is too slow."

Meera tilted her head, intrigued. "Alright, finance guru, any ideas?"

Arjun shrugged, "Not really, but I know we need something smarter."

Meera suddenly lit up. "You know, one of my friends is a Certified Financial Planner. Why don't we talk to him? He might have some suitable ideas for us."

Arjun chuckled, "Great! Call your expert friend. Let's make this money work harder than we do!"

With that decision, the couple was ready to explore professional suggestion to make their dream wedding a financial success. 😊

# A Wedding Fund Conversation with a Certified Financial Planner

Here's where the real fun begins. Meera, a close friend and super organized planner, picked up the phone and called none other than... me! Yes, me, the Certified Financial Planner. You might be thinking, "Wait, they called you?" Yep, they did! With a cup of coffee in hand and wedding plans in their minds, Meera and Arjun came straight to my office, ready to take control of their finances.

After a bit of chit-chat about their wedding goals (and my comments on how Indian weddings are turning into movie sets), we got down to business.

"So, what do you think we should do?" Meera asked, eager to make some smart financial moves.

I didn't waste time. **"Let's put that ₹10,00,000 to work by investing it in liquid mutual funds and add an SIP of ₹40,000 every month to the same liquid funds to help you reach your goal of ₹15,00,000."**

Arjun, being the curious one, furrowed his brows and asked, "Wait, wait! What exactly is a liquid mutual fund? And why not invest in equity mutual funds instead? Equity invests in stocks, right? That could give us bigger returns, right?"

I chuckled, leaned back in my chair, and said, "Yes, equity mutual funds can give you great returns, but here's the thing: You're saving for a wedding that's happening in one year. Equity mutual funds are best suited for goals that are more than 4 years away. Equity is a bit like a rollercoaster ride—you can make big gains, but there's also a chance of falling flat. And you definitely don't want your wedding fund turning into an IPL match where you're constantly checking the score!"

Liquid mutual funds, on the other hand, are one of the best alternatives to a savings account. You can expect around 6% to 6.5% per annum. They simply invest in short-term bonds, treasury bills, commercial papers, etc., so your money will be safe and grow steadily.

Arjun, still a bit confused, asked, "But if equity can give us more money, why not go for that? I mean, I want to travel to Europe after the wedding too!"

I smiled and said, "That's the spirit! We'll definitely plan for your Europe trip with equity funds, provided you invest for a minimum of 4 years. But for the wedding fund, let's stick to something safer. Think of liquid funds like a steady, reliable curd rice meal— just safe and easy to digest."

Arjun laughed at that, and then I asked, "Okay, but when's the wedding happening?"

Meera smiled and said, "We haven't fixed the exact date yet, but it'll be sometime between April and May next year."

I nodded and said, "Perfect timing! With liquid mutual funds, we've got just the right investment strategy for this short-term goal. We'll invest ₹10,00,000 safely, and the SIP of ₹40,000 every month into a liquid fund will make sure you hit your ₹15,00,000 target."

**The Wedding: Simplicity Meets Elegance**
With **₹15,60,000** in hand—thanks to the **6.5%** return on their liquid mutual fund investment over one year—Meera and Arjun planned their wedding thoughtfully:

- **Venue:** ₹4.5 lakhs for a charming garden wedding with a breezy outdoor vibe ("Chandeliers vendam, vaanam podhum! (No chandeliers needed, the sky is enough!)").

- **Catering:** ₹6 lakhs for a delicious South Indian spread that delighted everyone ("Rasam is always better than ravioli!").

- **Decor:** ₹1 lakh with DIY crafts and creative contributions from cousins.

- **Photography:** ₹3 lakhs, because candid shots are a must!

- Meera opted for a stunning ₹40,000 lehenga, while Arjun rocked a sharp ₹25,000 suit.

**The Afterparty: Debt-Free Bliss**

Their wedding turned out to be everything they dreamed of—intimate, elegant, and stress-free. Best of all, they didn't need to borrow a single rupee, and their parents were equally proud.

As a bonus, they even had **₹45,000** left from their wedding fund, which they used for a mini honeymoon to Pondicherry. Arjun quipped, "Bali illa, Pondy pothum! (No Bali, Pondy is enough!)"

**Takeaways: Weddings Need Heart, Not Hype**

- **Debt-Free is the Way to Be:** Meera and Arjun showed that with careful planning and smart investments, big dreams can fit into smaller budgets.

- **Short-Term Goals, Long-Term Joy:** By using liquid funds and SIPs, they saved without sacrificing their lifestyle.

- **Family First:** They prioritized their parents' peace of mind and ensured no one felt financial strain.

- **Budgeting isn't limiting—it's liberating:** You can have a dream wedding without overspending if you prioritize what matters.

In the end, Meera and Arjun's wedding wasn't just a celebration of love, but a perfect example of how goal-based financial planning can help you achieve your dreams without compromising your financial health.

**Remember, it's not about how much you spend; it's about the love and joy you share:** Wouldn't you agree?

❖ *From **March 2019 to April 2020**, the Liquid Fund category delivered a return of **6.5%**. This is why we used **6.5%** in the illustration. However, this does not guarantee that you will receive the same returns in the future, as liquid fund performance depends on prevailing interest rate scenarios. Realistically, you can expect returns in the range of 6% to 6.5% based on current market conditions.*

# Case Study 2

## Saving for a European Honeymoon

Meera and Arjun, the dynamic duo, had it all figured out—well, almost! After their wedding was set, the excitement of tying the knot was soon replaced with the next big dream: a **European honeymoon**! The only issue? Their **salary** which was more than enough for a great wedding, especially since they already had ₹10,00,000 in savings, but not so much for flights, hotels, croissants in Paris, and gondola rides in Venice.

Meera, always the organized planner, didn't want to compromise. She had one rule: no borrowing, no debt, and definitely no using credit cards for their dream vacation. So, what was the solution? A bit of **smart financial planning**, of course! And that's where I came in.

**The Plan to European Dream**

We sat down for a strategy session (with a side of masala chai, obviously), and after some back-and-forth, we came up with a plan. The goal: **Save ₹8,00,000** for their honeymoon in Europe within four years. Here's the calculation:

- **Current cost for 2 people** (including flights): ₹6,00,000

- **Estimated inflation**: 7% per year

- **Projected cost after 4 years**: ₹8,00,000

The breakdown:

- **Target Fund**: ₹8,00,000

- **Investment Strategy**: Equity mutual funds (yes, you have 4 years, so it's worth considering equity mutual funds)

- **Monthly SIP**: ₹14,000 (Assuming 11% returns, a practical assumption for 4-year period)

## The Investment: Equity Funds Are the Real Hero

Now, Arjun wasn't exactly sold on the idea of waiting for 4 years. He said, "Wait, four years? That's way too long! Why not just go now? We can use a credit card and pay it off later."

Meera, always the voice of reason, looked at him and replied, "It's better to wait and enjoy the trip fully without worrying about EMIs, Arjun. Trust me, a little patience will pay off. We'll save and invest wisely, and when we get there, we won't have to think about the bills afterward."

I chimed in, "Exactly! Think of it like this—equity funds are your ticket to making that trip a reality. Sure, there's some risk, but you have 4 years for the investment to grow. It's like a slow-burn story—just like how a good old masala chai takes time to brew."

**The Journey: Sip, Save, and Relax**

Meera and Arjun committed to putting ₹14,000 every month into their SIP in equity mutual funds for the next 4 years. Arjun kept asking, "What if we could go sooner?" But Meera stayed firm: "We'll go later, but we'll go **debt-free**, Arjun."

Meanwhile, Arjun and Meera enjoyed a lot of short trips, movies, concerts, early morning rides, and even a few midnight dinners (only sometimes, because Arjun, being the health-conscious person he is, wouldn't allow them too often!). They made the most of their time together, with the excitement of their European trip always in the back of their minds, building anticipation for the adventure that lay ahead.

And so, they stuck to their plan, month after month. I kept reassuring them: "Remember, with equity mutual funds, your investment is like that dream vacation—exciting, sometimes volatile, but worth it in the end. And with 4 years on your side, you'll have more time to ride out market ups and downs."

## The Reward: Europe, Here We Come!

Fast forward 4 years, and guess what? Meera and Arjun hit their ₹8,00,000 goal. Their equity investments had grown as expected, and they were ready to board the flight to Europe. No credit card bills, no EMIs, just a full-on, **stress-free European adventure**.

Arjun couldn't help but smile, "I'll admit it now, Meera. Waiting was worth it. Bali had to wait for later, but Europe… well, we're definitely doing it right!"

**Takeaways from This Case Study**

- **Patience Pays Off:** Meera and Arjun showed that sometimes waiting is the smartest financial move. With equity mutual funds and SIPs, their 4-year plan turned into a fully-funded European trip, debt-free!

- **Smart Investments Can Fund Big Dreams:** Even on a **decent salary**, planning and saving through equity mutual funds helped them make a dream vacation a reality.

- **Start Saving Early:** The couple showed that when you're saving for big goals, **the sooner you start**, the less stress you'll have when the time comes.

- **Debt-Free is the Way to Be:** Don't let loans and EMIs ruin the fun. Saving smartly now means more freedom and peace of mind later.

---

**The Final Thought:**

Whether you're sipping **chai in Chennai** or **wine in Italy**, remember—smart financial planning lets you enjoy life without the debt hangover. And who knows? With patience and consistency, your dream vacation could be closer than you think. Just ask Meera and Arjun—they'll tell you: It's all worth the wait!

# Case Study 3

## How Priya Got Her Dream Home Before 35

Meet Priya: The Marketing Genius with a Dream Home Vision

Priya is 29, a marketing manager with a knack for crafting the perfect pitch and a love for spontaneous weekend trips. Her monthly salary of ₹85,000 was just enough to cover everything—living the city life, paying the bills, etc. But deep down, Priya had one big goal: to buy her own home before she turned 35.

You see, Priya has a plan that's a little different from most people. She's single, and she's not just thinking about buying a house for the sake of it. No, Priya had a mission. **She was determined to own her own house before she even thought about getting married.**

"I don't want to be the one asking, 'Do you have a house?'" Priya would say with a wink. "I want to be the one telling my future partner, 'I have my own house, don't worry about it.'" It was her **dream**—and she was determined to make it happen. But how? She needed a strategy, and she wasn't going to rely on just good luck or a hefty salary raise. Priya knew that to turn this dream into reality, she needed to be smart, strategic, and *a little* adventurous.

## The Wake-Up Call: Dream Home, Real Goals

One weekend, as Priya sat in a cozy café sipping her cappuccino (with a side of guilt-free chocolate cake), reality struck her. She had been saving, sure, but saving alone wasn't going to get her to her dream home. It was time to take things up a notch.

Priya wasn't one to let inspiration slip away, so she grabbed her phone, opened the calculator app (no fancy spreadsheets here), and started crunching numbers. Here's what she found:

- **Current average cost of a 1200 sqft house in her desired area of Chennai:** ₹1.5 Crore

- **Assumed growth rate for the next 6 years (until she's 35):** 6% annually

- **Future value of the 1200 sqft apartment:** ₹2.10 Crores

Priya planned to make a **20% down payment**, which meant she needed to accumulate approximately **₹40,00,000** in 6 years.

That was her goal—she needed to accumulate ₹40 lakh for the down payment in **6 years**.

Priya stared at the numbers and thought, *Okay, now what? How am I going to do this?*

At first, Priya was completely clueless about how to make her money grow. Sure, she knew how to set a budget (especially when it came to *justifying* a new pair of shoes), but when it came to investing for something as big as a home, she had no idea where to start. Stocks? Bonds? Mutual funds? It all sounded like a different language.

She needed help. A plan. Something that wasn't just about saving but also growing her money in a smart way.

**The Call from Arjun: "Time for SIPs!"**

Luckily, Priya's close friend Arjun—who had just married Meera—called her one evening to catch up. As they chatted, Priya couldn't help but tease Arjun a bit. "So, tell me, how's married life? All roses and candle-lit dinners, or are you already planning for the next big thing—like, say, a new house?"

Arjun laughed and replied, "Well, speaking of big plans, we're gearing up for our Europe trip soon! And I gotta say, the way we managed it all was thanks to the suggestions I got from a financial planner. You remember the wedding expenses, right? He helped us manage all that, and now we're using his help for this trip too. You should totally talk to him.”

Priya was intrigued. She was planning to buy a house, but she had no clue how to go about investing for that big goal. So, Arjun continued, “Trust me, Priya, he’s good. He’ll help you figure this out. If he can make my wedding and European vacation work, I’m sure he can do some suggestions for your home plans too.”

**Now readers, I can hear the voice in your mind: “overbuild up ah iruke” (Looks like overbuild up))** *Lol ,* 😂 *I get it, I get it. It’s like making myself sound like the movie hero, right? but just my little wish. That’s why my friend, I can understand… leave it, leave it.”*

### The First Conversation: “SIPs, What's That?”

The next day, Priya gave me a call. I could sense the excitement in her voice as she explained her dream of buying a house. “I need to buy a house in 6 years! But I have no idea how to make that happen,” she admitted.

I smiled. It was exactly the kind of challenge I love. "Alright, Priya. Let's break it down," I said. "You have to save₹40 lakh 6 years. Since you have 6 years time period I suggest you to make SIP's in equity mutual funds

Priya paused. "SIPs?" she asked, sounding like I'd just introduced her to some secret society.

"Yup, SIPs! They stand for Systematic Investment Plans. It's like a regular exercise routine, but for your money. You invest a fixed amount every month in mutual funds. Over time, your money grows with the power of **compounding**.

Still, Priya wasn't entirely convinced. "But equity mutual funds invest in stocks right? isn't that risky? I don't want to lose money while waiting for my dream house."

I told her: "Priya, equity mutual funds have historically given returns of about **12% over 5 to 6 years.** Of course, returns can vary, but with 6 years in play, you'll have time for those ups and downs to balance out."

## Crunching the Numbers: SIP Strategy for Priya's Dream Home

We worked together to figure out how much Priya would need to invest monthly to reach her ₹40 lakh goal in 6 years. After a few calculations, the magic number came out to be **₹40,000** every month.

At that point, Priya's mind went into overdrive. Here's a peek into what was going on inside her head:

1. **First Thought:** "Wait... ₹40,000? That's a huge chunk of my salary! I can't just give up my brunches, can I?"

2. **Second Thought:** "But what about my spontaneous weekend trips to Goa? Ugh, I need to think this through."

3. **Third Thought:** "Wait, this could work if I keep it up consistently. It's not about depriving myself. It's about balancing fun and smart savings!"

## Priya's New Financial Plan: Balancing Fun and Saving

Her monthly salary was ₹85,000. After covering the usual expenses—rent, groceries, OTT subscriptions, and EMI's —Priya realized she could still comfortably set aside ₹40,000 every month for SIPs without feeling like she was sacrificing everything.

## Priya's SIP Journey: Growing Her Wealth (and Her Confidence)

With her SIP plan in place, Priya set up her monthly investments. Month after month, she deposited ₹40,000 into her chosen equity mutual funds, watching her money grow.

There were times when the market dipped, and Priya panicked. "Should I stop investing? What if I lose everything?" she'd ask.

I'd remind her: "Remember, Priya, investing in equity funds is like a marathon, not a sprint. The market may fluctuate, but with time, your investments will grow. Stick to the plan, and you'll reach your goal."

Sure enough, Priya stayed the course. Her ₹40,000 SIPs added up, and the power of compounding worked its magic. Over the next few years, her investment grew steadily, and soon, Priya was closer to her ₹40 lakh target than she'd ever imagined.

**The Grand Reveal: Priya Buys Her Dream Home**

When Priya turned 35, she had a solid ₹40 lakh in her mutual fund portfolio. She had stuck to the plan, balanced fun with saving, and avoided the temptation to splurge on unnecessary things.

She was ready to take the leap into homeownership.

But there's more to this story. In the 6 years since she'd started her SIPs, Priya's life had transformed. Her salary had grown from ₹85,000 to ₹1,50,000 per month. At the start, she'd been investing nearly **50%** of her salary into her SIPs. But over the years, as her income grew, her allocation percentage naturally reduced to around **25%** of her monthly salary.

The best part? Her SIPs had already grown with the power of compounding, putting her in a much stronger position than she'd ever imagined.

On the day she turned 35, Priya walked into her dream home with the keys in her hand, ready to make it her own. She didn't need to ask the groom, "Do you have a house?" because she was the one proudly saying, "I have my own house, thank you!"

Her dream was no longer just a wish—it was her reality. All the hard work, consistency, and smart investing had paid off. Priya had done it, and she had done it on **her terms.**

**What Priya's Story Teaches Us:**

1. **Start Early:** Priya began investing early and gave her money time to grow. The earlier you start, the easier it is to build wealth over time.

2. **Consistency is Key:** Regular investments (like Priya's ₹40,000 SIP) add up over time. It's not about big lumps of money, but about consistency.

3. **Balance is Everything:** Priya didn't give up on her fun. She found a way to balance saving with enjoying life.

4. **Patience Pays Off:** Even when the market fluctuated, Priya stuck to her plan. The long-term results were worth the wait.

5. **Smart Planning Works:** With the right strategy, Priya was able to save for her dream home without giving up her lifestyle.

**The Bottom Line:**

Priya's story shows that with a little financial planning, **you too can reach your dream**

**goals**—whether it's a home, a car, or a vacation in Paris. SIPs aren't just about saving money; they're about making your money work hard for you. So, are you ready to start your journey towards your financial goals?

# Case study 4
## Sanjay, the Car, and the Wedding Wisdom

A few months ago, I found myself at yet another family wedding, navigating plates of biryani and gulab jamuns while dodging overly enthusiastic aunties asking, "So, when's your turn?" For a moment, I froze, then replied, "Aunty, I'm already married! If I do another one, my wife will turn me into a gulab jamun!"

The aunties burst into laughter, but just then, I noticed Sanjay—my cousin's friend—walking up to me. Sanjay, just 24 years old, had started his career as a software developer only a few months back. He was earning ₹40,000 a month—a decent starting salary for someone fresh in the workforce. But today, he had something on his mind that he just couldn't shake.

"Anna, I'm planning to buy a sedan car," he said, his face lighting up with excitement.

"Nice, what's the plan?" I asked.

"It's ₹15 lakhs. My dad said he'd help with ₹3 lakhs as a down payment, and I'll manage the rest through EMI—around ₹20,000 a month," he said confidently.

I paused, calculating in my head. "Wait, ₹20,000 EMI? Your salary is ₹40,000, right? That's 50% of your monthly income!"

Sanjay shrugged. "Yeah, but it's my dream car, and I can make it work."

**The Smarter Route: 3 Years to Financial Stability**

I smiled. "Look, Sanjay, I get it. Cars are amazing, and the feeling of owning one is unbeatable. But let me share some advice, not as a financial planner, but as a guy who's seen enough people struggle with money.

If your EMI eats up 50% of your salary, what will you do about rent, food, or even those impulse Zomato orders?"

He nodded hesitantly. "Okay, so what do you suggest?"

I leaned in, speaking over the sound of the dhol. "Here's a better plan:

1. **Start with Your Dad's ₹3 Lakhs**: Invest this amount instead of using it as an immediate down payment.

2. **Add ₹9,500 SIP Every Month**: Invest ₹9,500 monthly in a **Balanced Advantage Fund (BAF)** and a **Multi-Asset Fund.** These are investment options designed to give you steady growth:

- ○ **Balanced Advantage Fund**: Dynamically shifts between equity and debt, depending on market conditions, to provide stable returns while minimizing risk.

- ○ **Multi-Asset Fund**: Invests across different asset classes like equity, debt, and gold, spreading risk and creating diversification.
  **What You Can Expect**

- ○ **With ₹3,00,000 as an initial investment and ₹9,500 SIPs over 3 years, you can aim for a corpus of ₹8,00,000, assuming a 10% annual return.**

3. **Car Cost in 2027**:
   Assuming the car's price grows by 5% annually, the ₹15 lakh car will cost around ₹17.5 lakhs in three years.

4. **A Bigger Down Payment (45%)**:
   Use the ₹8 lakhs to make a 45% down payment, reducing your loan amount to ₹9.3 lakhs.

5. **Manageable EMI**:
   With a loan of ₹9.3 lakhs, your EMI for 7 years at 10% interest would be around ₹15,000—a reasonable 25% of your salary (assuming you'll be earning ₹60,000 after 3 years).

## Why Waiting Makes Sense

"Look, Sanjay," I continued, "let's assume you're 27 years old now with some experience managing your salary and expenses. If your EMI took up just within 25% of your salary, I'd say go for the car loan without a second thought."

That's because life is 80% psychology and 20% math. If owning this car is your dream, it's okay to prioritize it. But at this stage, you're just starting your career. You're still new to handling a salary and figuring out your financial priorities.

The first three years of your salary journey are crucial. It's the time to learn how to manage money—what your priorities are, where you spend, and what genuinely brings you joy. This clarity comes with time and experience. So, my advice is to hold off on the car plan for now."

## Sanjay's Realization

Sanjay looked thoughtful. "Three years feels like a long time to hold off."

I laughed. "Sanjay, doesn't *2021 to 2024* feel like it was just yesterday? That's how fast time flies. Trust me, when 2027 comes around, you'll thank yourself for waiting. By then, you'll have your car, peace of mind, and financial stability. No stress about tying up half your salary in EMIs."

After a pause, he smiled. "Fine, Anna, I'll wait for three years. But when I buy that car, you're coming for the first drive!"

"Deal," I said with a laugh. "And you're treating me to biryani!"

## The Takeaway

The moral of the story? Dreams and desires are important, but so is managing your money wisely. Patience pays off, and sometimes, waiting just a little longer can help you get what you want without putting your future at risk. So, if you're feeling like Sanjay and want to buy a car or do something big, just remember: don't let the EMI eat away at your dreams!

Because, as I always say, life isn't just about the car you drive—it's about driving your life with financial freedom.

# Case Study 5

## How Anjali Quit Her Job to Start a Bakery

So, let me tell you about **Anjali**. This story happened back in *2019*—a friend of my neighbour who had a **big dream** to open her own bakery. Imagine this: she's working as a **finance manager**, earning ₹75,000 a month. Life looks sorted, right? But Anjali's mind isn't on balance sheets and audits

Anjali was dreaming about **frosting cakes**, **whipping up cookies**, and **baking pastries** that make people go *"OMG, this is amazing!"* 😋 She imagined the **aroma of freshly baked goodies** filling the air and customers walking in for that unforgettable croissant or cake.

Now here's the catch—starting a bakery isn't exactly *pocket change*. She figured she needed ₹15,00,000 to make her dream a reality. Luckily, she'd saved ₹3,00,000 from her salary Her plan? Use the ₹3,00,000 and take a loan of ₹12,00,000 for the rest.

She excitedly shared this idea with me at a metro station—**total coincidence**, by the way. I listened, then said, *"Anjali, I totally understand your excitement, but taking a loan isn't the best option right now. Without a solid plan, it could cause a lot of stress."*

She looked confused. *"Why not?"*

*"Well,"* I said, *"Have you thought about how long it'll take for your bakery to break even and cover your living expenses? What if things take longer than planned? A business is exciting, but starting one with a loan and no backup can turn risky really fast."*

Then I added, *"But don't worry. I've got a plan where you don't need a loan, and you can still have peace of mind about your monthly expenses. **Hold your plan for five years,** and I assure you you'll be in a much better position."*

Her jaw dropped. ***"Five years?! Are you serious? I can't wait that long! Why would I?"***

I smiled. *"Anjali, I get it. But hear me out—you're starting this bakery to live your dream and do what you love. If money issues crop up, it could mess everything up. Let me explain how five years can change everything for you."*

**The Plan**

**"Invest that ₹3,00,000 into equity mutual funds**—split between a Large & Midcap Fund and a Multicap Fund. Assuming a **12% return**, this will grow to ₹5,28,000 in five years. *Use this for your living expenses when you finally start your business in 2024.*

What's your monthly living expense today, Anjali?"

She replied, *"Around ₹40,000 per month."*

"Okay, factor in inflation at **6%**, and by 2024, you'd need ₹52,000 per month. That ₹5,28,000 will cover **10 months** of living expenses. So, for the first 10 months, you can focus on your bakery without stressing about monthly bills.

Now, for your business corpus—you said you need ₹15,00,000 today. With **6% annual inflation**, this will become ₹20,00,000 by 2024. Here's what you do: **Save ₹25,000 every month** from your ₹75,000 salary and invest it in equity mutual funds. At an expected **12% return**, you'll accumulate ₹20,00,000 in five years.

By 2024, you'll have the full ₹20,00,000 for your bakery and ₹5,28,000 for your living expenses. **No loans, no stress**—just you, your bakery, and a whole lot of pastries."

Anjali paused and asked, *"What if I use this ₹3,00,000 now to cover my ₹40,000 monthly expenses for seven months and take a ₹15,00,000 loan for the business?"*

I smiled. *"Anjali, I get where you're coming from. But think about this—if you take a loan, you'll have EMIs to pay. How will you manage that? You're planning this bakery to live a **happy, purposeful life**. I don't want money troubles ruining your peace of mind. That's why I suggest avoiding loans. Do your dream work, but do it peacefully."*

She sighed. *"Okay, I get it. But aren't equity mutual funds risky? I'm a little hesitant."*

"Anjali," I said, *"you're willing to risk quitting your job and taking a ₹15,00,000 loan for your bakery. So, clearly, you're okay with taking risks. **Equity** *__mutual funds__ are good option for a five-year horizon. Trust me, it's the smarter move."*

Finally, she agreed, and we started the process the very next day.

## Fast Forward to 2024: A Sweet Success

Five years later, **Anjali's bakery opened its doors.** Not only did she have her ₹20,00,000 corpus ready, but her ₹3,00,000 had grown into ₹5,28,000. This gave her the **breathing space** to focus on her passion without worrying about money.

And guess what? She baked the most drool-worthy brownies and croissants, just like she imagined. Customers kept coming back for more!

But here's the best part: during those five years, **Anjali didn't just sit and wait.** She took the opportunity to **learn as much as she could** about running a bakery. She read books, watched tutorials, and even **worked part-time in a bakery** to get hands-on experience. This gave her valuable insights into the business, from managing customers to learning baking tricks she hadn't even imagined. It was a **game-changer**. By the time she was ready to open her own bakery, she had all the knowledge and real-world experience she needed to run it smoothly.

**Key Takeaways from Anjali's Story**

1. **Patience Pays**: Waiting and planning allowed Anjali to start her dream business stress-free.

2. **Inflation Awareness**: Factoring in inflation ensured she was financially prepared for future costs.

3. **Smart Investments**: A thoughtful strategy replaced the need for risky loans.

4. **No EMI, No Stress: Being debt-free allowed Anjali to focus entirely on her passion.**

5. **Learning Never Stops**: Even while waiting, you can **learn and grow** in your field. Gaining experience is as important as building funds.

**Moral of the story?** *Hitting pause on your dream doesn't mean stopping—it means setting yourself up to dream bigger and better.*

Today, **Anjali's bakery journey** is as sweet as her treats, and she wouldn't have it any other way. 😊

# Case study 6

## Anirudh's Escape: Breaking Free from the EMI Trap

It was a regular Friday afternoon when I got a call from Anirudh, my close school friend. His voice sounded a little different today, not the usual carefree tone. "Bro, can you meet me? I need

your help with something serious," he said. Curious, I agreed to meet him at my office.

As he entered, I could see the stress in his eyes. He slumped into the chair and let out a deep sigh. "Man, I'm drowning here," he said, rubbing his forehead. "I earn ₹1,10,000 every month, but guess what? 65% of it goes straight into EMIs, another 30% goes towards household expenses, and I'm left with just ₹5,500. That's it! How am I supposed to enjoy life? I can't even plan a dinner or hang out with friends without feeling guilty. What do I do?"

I could immediately tell this was more than just a 'numbers' problem. It was about the stress that comes with living paycheck to paycheck, even when your income seems like enough. I sat back in my chair and smiled, knowing exactly where to begin.

## The Dream of Financial Freedom: Step 1 – Stop the Panic Mode

"Okay, Anirudh, let's take a deep breath. First of all—relax," I said. "Let's get out of the panic zone and think through this step by step. You're clearly doing well for yourself, but it's the way the money is being spent that's causing the stress. You've got 65% of your salary going into EMIs. That's a huge chunk. And while household expenses are important, that 30% is more or less under control. So, what's left? Just ₹5,500—hardly enough to breathe, right?"

"Exactly!" he said, nodding. "I can barely get my head above water, forget about enjoying life!"

I smiled. "I get it. But we can definitely fix this. I'm not suggesting you take on a second job or start selling your old stuff on OLX. We'll do this the smart way."

## Idea 1: Redeem Investments to Reduce EMI

"First things first—look at your investments. Do you have any Fixed Deposits or Mutual Fund investments sitting around?"

He looked up, surprised. "I do, but I've been holding onto them for long-term growth. Don't want to touch them."

I chuckled. "I get that. But here's the deal: If you have FDs or mutual funds, it might be worth considering redeeming them to pay off some of your loans, especially the high-interest ones. By settling loans with higher interest rates, your EMI will drop significantly. That'll free up more money for other things. Yes, you'll be using some of your long-term savings, but think of this as debt-freedom insurance. That peace of mind is priceless."

Anirudh's face lit up. "But I'll miss out on all that investment growth!"

I raised a finger. "Not if it's taking a toll on your lifestyle. If the stress of high EMIs is stopping you from living your life, then it's worth making this move. Free yourself from debt first. We'll talk about wealth creation later, once you're breathing easier."

## Idea 2: Sell the Car – Seriously!

I leaned forward and looked Anirudh straight in the eye. "Now, let's talk about your car."

He stared at me in disbelief. "What about my car?"

"Well, I know you don't use it much—only about three times a month, right?"

"Yeah, it just sits in the parking lot most of the time," he admitted.

I could sense a shift in his mind. "Exactly. And that car loan you're carrying? If you sell the car, you'll not only get rid of that loan but also free up a chunk of cash. I know it sounds a bit drastic, but hear me out. You're not using it enough to justify keeping it."

He looked at me, still unsure. "But, I bought it for ₹10,00,000! It's probably worth ₹8,00,000 now!"

I laughed. "Life's 80% psychology, 20% math, Anirudh. That car's value isn't about the numbers—it's about the relief you'll get when you sell it and say goodbye to that car loan.

Sometimes, holding onto things for the wrong reasons can be a bigger cost to your peace of mind. You'll have more freedom and less stress. I promise you, the psychological benefit will outweigh the financial loss."

Anirudh paused, then slowly nodded. "Okay, I get it. I think I can do that. But I'll miss the drives!"

"Trust me, Anirudh, the relief you'll feel when the loan is gone will be worth it."

"Correct me if I'm wrong," I added, "you're paying ₹15,000 per month on that car loan, right?"

Anirudh nodded. "Yeah, that's right."

"Well, by selling the car and settling the loan, you'll be saving that ₹15,000 every month. That's an extra ₹15,000 you can put towards something else—like investing in your future or just having some fun!"

**Idea 3: Debt Consolidation – Let's Simplify Things**

"Now, let's look at another option: Debt Consolidation. You've got several loans with EMIs totaling ₹40,000 a month (excluding your housing loan EMI of ₹31,500), right? If you add up all your outstanding loans, it comes to around ₹18,00,000."

"Yeah, it's a bit much to juggle all at once," Anirudh said, sighing.

"So, here's the solution," I said, leaning back in my chair. "If your CIBIL score and income track record are good, you could consolidate all your loans into one. You could take out a personal loan from another bank at a relatively lower interest rate—say, around 12% for seven years. By doing this, you could reduce your EMI from ₹40,000 to ₹31,000. That gives you an extra ₹9,000 every month!"

Anirudh's eyes widened. "Wait, what? That's ₹9,000 more in my pocket every month? How is that possible?"

"It's simple math, my friend. With one consolidated loan, you're lowering your EMI burden, which gives you more cash flow. You can use that extra ₹9,000 to save, invest, or even enjoy a night out without worrying about your finances."

**Conclusion: Time for Some Smart Decisions**

"Anirudh, here's the plan: Once you have some breathing room, start building an emergency fund. Aim for at least three to six months of living expenses saved up. Also, get some term and health insurance coverage—it's essential for protecting your future."

"I'll go home and discuss the options you suggested with my wife and let you know," Anirudh said, nodding thoughtfully. "I'm feeling more confident now that I have a clear plan to get back on track..

"Great! And remember, the key is to keep your EMIs manageable. The less you owe, the more you can build for the future. Trust me, life without those crushing EMIs is way more satisfying than anything you'll find in a car loan or credit card bill."

Anirudh left my office feeling relieved and optimistic, ready to take charge of his finances and live life on his own terms. After all, it's not just about earning well—it's about making that money work for you!

# Case study 7

## Rajesh's Housing Loan Dilemma: Pay Off or Invest?

So, last week, I was at Toastmasters, giving a speech about **financial independence** (yeah, I was on fire, if I may say so myself). After the session, as usual, people came up with all sorts of questions, but there was one person, Rajesh, who really had me thinking. Rajesh is a 40-year-old senior software engineer, and he came up to me looking a little puzzled.

"Hey, that was a really good talk," Rajesh said. "But I'm stuck with this question, and I don't know who to ask. I have a housing loan of ₹1 crore with an 8.5% interest rate. My current EMI is ₹86,000, and the loan tenure is 20 years," Rajesh began. "After covering all my expenses, I have an extra ₹15,000 every month. Should I use this extra money to increase my EMI and pay off the loan faster, or should I invest it in mutual funds? Which option would be better in the long run?"

I could tell he was looking for a solid answer, so I smiled and said, "Rajesh, that's a **great** question. But I'm a bit hungry after all this speaking. How about we grab lunch? We can chat about it at **Geetham Restaurant.**

He laughed. "Sounds like a plan! Let's get to it."

**At Geetham Restaurant... Let's Break It Down**

Over lunch, I took a moment to explain both options carefully. Here's how I broke it down for Rajesh:

**Option 1: Increase EMI by ₹15,000 and Pay Off the Loan Faster**

I started by explaining the first option, "So Rajesh, if you decide to use that ₹15,000 extra to increase your EMI, here's what would happen:

- **Loan Tenure**: Your loan tenure would reduce significantly, from **20 years** to about **14 years**.

- **Interest Savings**: You'd save a huge chunk of money—approximately **₹35.09 lakhs** in interest over the term of the loan.

- **Early Payoff**: This means you'd be debt-free about **6 years earlier** than initially planned.

The obvious benefit here is that you would clear your loan faster, and you won't be stuck with this debt hanging over you. It's a great option if you're the type who's more comfortable without outstanding debt."

Rajesh nodded thoughtfully. "That sounds like a solid plan. Paying off the loan faster could reduce my stress, but... what's the other option?"

**Option 2: Invest ₹15,000 in Equity Mutual Funds**

I smiled and continued, "Now let's look at the second option. Instead of putting that ₹15,000 into your EMI, you could **invest it in equity**

**mutual funds**. Assuming **12% average return**, here's how that ₹15,000 would work for you:

- Over the course of **14 years** (which is how long it would take to repay the loan if you increased the EMI), that ₹15,000 per month could grow into a **corpus of ₹62 lakhs**.

Imagine having ₹62 lakhs after 14 years! This gives you the potential to create wealth that you could use for other goals—like retirement, your kids' education, or even buying a second property.

While the market does carry risks, historically, **equity mutual funds have outperformed loan interest savings**, especially if you stay invested for the long term."

## The Key Comparison

I took a moment to compare the two options for Rajesh: "So, in a nutshell:

- **Increasing your EMI** would **save you money** on interest (₹35.09 lakhs), and you'd be debt-free **sooner**.

- **Investing in mutual funds** could provide **higher returns and you'll accumulate good wealth** (₹62 lakhs )but with some market risks involved.

Rajesh scratched his head, clearly deep in thought. "But what if I want both? I mean, I'd love to pay off the loan faster, but I also want to invest for my future."

## A Hybrid Approach

I grinned. "Great point! You don't have to choose just one. You can do a **hybrid approach**—split the ₹15,000 between paying off the loan and investing in mutual funds. You could allocate ₹7,500 towards increasing your EMI, which will help you pay off your loan faster, and use the other ₹7,500 to invest in equity mutual funds. This way, you're reducing your debt while also building a financial corpus.

Rajesh, if debt doesn't stress you out,  focusing on investments could help you build wealth alongside owning your home.  While equity mutual funds carry some market risks, they also offer the potential for better returns than the interest savings from repaying your loan faster in long term.

In the long run,  you could own your home and have a strong financial corpus with investments. However,  if being debt-free sooner is a priority for you,  then increasing your EMI would make sense.  It all depends on your comfort with risk and your financial goals.

**Rajesh's Decision**

After thinking it over, Rajesh put his spoon down and looked at me with a decisive smile. "You know what? I'm going to go with the **mutual fund**

**route.** I'm okay with handling the debt for a bit longer if it means I have the potential to grow my wealth substantially. The idea of having ₹62 lakhs in 14 years is pretty compelling."

## The Final Takeaway

So, what can we learn from Rajesh's decision?

1. **Increasing the EMI**: This option reduces your debt faster and saves you money on interest. It's a great choice if becoming debt-free quickly is a priority for you.

2. **Investing in Mutual Funds**: If you're comfortable with the risk, equity mutual funds offer better long-term growth potential compared to the savings you get from paying off the loan faster.

3. **Hybrid Strategy**: If you want the best of both worlds—reduce debt and build wealth—splitting the ₹15,000 is a smart choice.

## Rajesh's Path Forward

In the end, Rajesh made a smart decision: he chose to **invest ₹15,000 every month** in equity mutual funds, all while continuing to pay off his loan with his original EMI. It's a win-win situation—he's building his wealth and still managing his home loan responsibly.

**The Moral of the Story?**

The right option depends on your goals, risk tolerance, and financial comfort level. **If debt isn't stressing you out**, you might benefit more from investing and letting your money grow. But, if you're someone who sleeps better knowing you're debt-free, increasing your EMI could be the way to go.

In Rajesh's case, with his decision to invest, he's on the path to **financial growth** while still keeping his home loan manageable.

And now, whenever we meet for a follow-up chat, I always remind him to treat me for lunch at **Geetham** as a thanks for sorting out his financial strategy!

# Case Study 8

## Gopal's ₹1 Crore Term Insurance with Minimal Premiums Through Mutual Funds

One fine evening, Gopal, my childhood friend, came over to my house to personally hand me his wedding invitation. As soon as he stepped in, I greeted him with a big grin and teased, "Ah, Gopal! Only a few more days left to enjoy your freedom. Are you sure you want to give it all up?"

Gopal burst out laughing. "Look who's talking! The guy who's already lost his freedom!"

Hearing this, my wife, who was sitting nearby, shot me *the look*. You know, the one that says, *"Don't even try it."* I quickly straightened up and cleared my throat, pretending to adjust my watch. "Jokes apart, buddy, congratulations! You're entering an exciting phase of life."

## The Insurance Talk

As we sat down for tea, I casually slipped in, "By the way, Gopal, now that you're getting married, you should seriously think about getting term insurance."

Gopal, the practical guy that he is, raised an eyebrow. "Term insurance? I don't get it. It's like paying a premium every year and not getting anything back. Why not invest that money in equity mutual funds instead? I believe in the Indian market. It's growing, and the potential is huge!"

Gopal had been investing in mutual funds for a while, and I could see the returns he was talking about. Over the last four years, he had been investing ₹30,000 every month in an SIP in the funds I had suggested. He had already accumulated a whopping ₹19.4 lakh!

"Look at this," Gopal said, showing me his portfolio on his phone. "This is what I've earned by investing in the market! No returns with insurance. Mutual funds have treated me well."

## The Watchman Analogy

I smiled and nodded. "You're absolutely right, Gopal. But let me put things into perspective with a simple analogy. Imagine you've bought a beautiful house, and you've hired a watchman to keep it safe.

Now, at the end of the month, the watchman comes to you for his salary. Would you say, 'No, I won't pay you because no theft happened?'"

Gopal chuckled. "Well, no! The watchman still did his job, even though there was no break-in."

"Exactly!" I said. "Just like the watchman, term insurance is protection. It's not about getting something in return right away. It's about ensuring that if something unexpected happens, your family is taken care of. That's what protection is."

## Understanding the Value of Term Insurance

I could see Gopal was still unsure, so I continued, "Look, I totally understand that the idea of paying a premium and not getting anything tangible in return feels frustrating. But think of it this way: let's say you're getting a ₹1 crore term insurance for an annual premium of ₹35,000. Over the next 30 years, you would have paid ₹10.5 lakh in premiums, right?"

"Okay, that's true. But I'd rather invest that ₹35,000 every year," Gopal responded, still skeptical.

"I hear you, Gopal! But listen to this: Along with getting your ₹1 crore term insurance plan, start a ₹3,000 per month SIP in equity mutual funds. Assuming a 12% annual return, in 15 years, your investment would grow to ₹14 lakh.

"For the first 15 years, you'll pay the ₹35,000 annual insurance premium from your income. But once your mutual fund corpus reaches ₹14 lakh, move it to an aggressive hybrid mutual fund. From this, you can start withdrawing ₹35,000 annually to cover your insurance premiums for the next 15 years.

"And here's the best part: while you're withdrawing ₹35,000 each year, the remaining amount in your hybrid fund will continue to grow."

## The Power of Compounding

Gopal looked intrigued. "Wait, so my investments will not only handle the premiums but also keep growing?"

"Exactly!" I replied enthusiastically. "After 15 years, your ₹14 lakh corpus in the aggressive hybrid mutual fund, assuming a 10% annual return, would have grown to about ₹47 lakh—even with the ₹35,000 annual withdrawals for your insurance premiums. That's the power of compounding and smart financial planning."

"Now you've got your term insurance, and you're still growing your wealth!"

## The Final Realization

Gopal's eyes widened. "So, I get insurance, my premium is covered, and I still end up with a huge corpus? That's genius!"

"Exactly, Gopal! And if nothing happens to you, you've built up a nice financial cushion. And in case something does happen, your family is covered with ₹1 crore of insurance. It's a win-win, right?"

Gopal leaned back, clearly impressed. "You know, this actually makes sense now. I've been too focused on the returns from the market, but I never looked at the big picture. You've opened my eyes!"

We both laughed, and I could see that Gopal had finally understood the balance between protection and investment. Term insurance was never meant to generate returns—its role was to protect, and it was a crucial part of financial planning. Meanwhile, the investment strategy gave him both growth and security.

"So, what do you think now?" I asked.

"I'm definitely going to take your advice! I'll get term insurance, and I'll also continue my SIPs. Thanks for the great idea, buddy!" Gopal replied, his confidence in financial planning clearly growing.

And with that, Gopal left my house, not only with his wedding invitation but also with a new understanding of how to balance his financial goals. I couldn't help but smile as I thought, "Sometimes, a good analogy can really make a difference!"

# CASE STUDY 9

## The Auto Ride That Turned Into Financial Suggestion

It was one of those days when my car was giving me trouble—brake issues, to be specific. So, I had no choice but to rely on Ola to get to my client's place. I booked an auto, but the driver accepted and then canceled the ride twice!

Finally, one driver accepted my ride request but with a catch—he wanted an extra ₹100. I agreed, thinking, "A small price to pay for a smooth ride."

When I entered the auto, the driver, a middle-aged man, casually started chatting. He mentioned that, due to rising costs and his loan commitments, he had to ask for the extra ₹100. Now, as a financial planner, I was *dying* to dive into this conversation and find out more. So, I seized the opportunity—after all, we had a 25-minute ride ahead of us!

## The Dream Car and Auto Business Plans

I asked him, "So, tell me more about this extra ₹100 request. I'm curious." That's when he opened up. His name was Ramesh, and he told me that he loved cars more than autos. In fact, his dream was to buy a new car and become a car driver—he was even looking into driving outstation and doing private hire!

But here's where it got interesting. Ramesh wasn't just paying off a loan for his auto for the next five years—he had bigger plans. He said, "Once I finish paying this loan, I want to buy a car." But that's not all. He had inherited

₹5,00,000 from his grandfather after selling a piece of land, which was shared among 10 grandsons. Ramesh's plan was to use this money to buy a second-hand auto, rent it out, and earn extra income on the side.

While Ramesh's idea of investing in another auto to rent out seemed like a good way to make extra income, I started to see some risks. I told him, "Let's assume you buy an auto and rent it out. You'll be getting daily rent, right? But what if the driver stops showing up, or leaves the job? You'll be left without that second income. And after a few months or maybe a year, if you realize this idea isn't working, you'll end up selling the auto. But you know that you'll likely sell it for less than what you bought it for, right?" So, instead of taking that risk, I suggested he use his ₹5,00,000 more wisely.

## Here Comes the Financial Planner

Hearing this, I couldn't help myself. I had to step in and give him some suggestion. I started by asking, "Ramesh, do you have a dream car?"

He replied, "Yes, I've been eyeing a car that costs ₹12,00,000."

I nodded, "Let's assume inflation will push that car's price up by 6% annually. In five years, that car, or maybe an updated model, will cost around ₹16,00,000. Now, what if I told you that you could buy that car without taking out a loan?"

## The Investment Plan

Ramesh looked at me, puzzled. "But how?"

Invest it in equity mutual funds. Also, put ₹1,500 into a monthly SIP (Systematic Investment Plan). Assuming a 12% return on investment, in 5 years, your ₹5,00,000 would grow to ₹16,00,000! That's enough to buy your dream car without any loans."

Ramesh's eyes widened. "Wait, what's SIP? What are equity mutual funds?"

## Breaking Down SIP and Equity Mutual Funds

"Good question, Ramesh! SIP is a method of investing in mutual funds where you invest a fixed amount regularly, say ₹1,500 every month.

Over time, the money you invest grows, thanks to the power of compounding. Now, equity mutual funds are a pool of money from various investors that are managed by experts who invest in stocks—companies that have the potential to grow and perform well over time. These funds are designed for long-term growth."

Ramesh was still a little skeptical. "But sir, stocks are risky. What if I lose all my money?"

I smiled, "I understand your concern, Ramesh. But let me ask you this: Do you believe that India's economy is going to slow down in the next five years? Do you think your future and your kid's future will be at risk?"

"No, sir! I believe India is growing," he replied.

"Exactly," I said. "And that's the reason you shouldn't worry about investing in stocks. Stocks grow when the economy grows. You're not investing in individual companies—you're investing in the future of India. Plus, don't forget, the fund manager is the one making the decisions, not you. He's the expert. And 5 years is a good duration for investing in the market— long enough to ride out any bumps along the way. Many people have made excellent returns over time by investing in mutual funds."

## Closing the Deal

By now, we were almost at my client's place, and Ramesh was deep in thought. "This sounds good, sir, but I need to think about it," he said.

I handed him my visiting card and said, "Ramesh, if you're ever interested in taking the first step towards securing your financial future, give me a call. Me and my team will take care of everything. No worries."

To my surprise, that very evening, Ramesh called me back! He said, "Sir, I'm ready to invest in mutual funds."

And just like that, I had helped a man on his way to achieving his dream car—without the burden of debt.

So, the next time you're stuck in traffic or taking an auto ride, remember: financial advice can come from the most unexpected places!

**Key Takeaways from This Chapter:**

1. **Smart Financial Planning:** Sometimes, an immediate financial decision, like buying another auto for rent, may seem appealing, but it's important to evaluate the long-term risks. It's wise to look at more secure and profitable ways to use your savings.

2. **Utilizing Assets Wisely:** Instead of using inherited money for buying depreciating asset (like buying a second-hand auto), Ramesh could invest it in more potential, long-term avenues like mutual funds, which could grow his money over time.

3. **The Power of SIP and Mutual Funds:** By investing in mutual funds and contributing a small monthly amount through SIP (Systematic Investment Plan), Ramesh could accumulate enough funds to purchase his dream car in five years without any loans.

4. **Taking Advantage of India's Growth Story:** Ramesh's hesitation about equity mutual funds was based on the fear of market volatility, but the long-term potential of India's economy and its stock market growth makes it a compelling investment opportunity. Trusting professional fund managers with your money can help navigate this risk.

5. **Financial Discipline and Patience:** Planning for big goals like buying a car without debt requires patience and discipline. Using an SIP strategy over the years can help you achieve those goals without taking on financial burdens or unnecessary loans.

# Case Study 10

## Kishore's Salary Split: The Path to Smart Money Management

One fine day, Sanjay, my client who had come to me previously with his car-buying plan (Case Study 4), showed up at my office. This time, he wasn't alone. He had brought along his colleague Kishore, a fellow software developer. Both were the same age 24, earning a similar salary of ₹40,000 per month.

As soon as they settled down, Sanjay said, "This is my friend Kishore. He just started working six months ago, and I told him about how you helped me with my car plan. He's here for some suggestion too."

Kishore, with a mix of eagerness and hesitation, began, "I'm earning ₹40,000 a month, but honestly, I feel lost. I want to make sure I enjoy this money and make it work for me. But I also want to feel like ₹40,000 is a huge salary. How can I find that balance?"

His approach intrigued me. Most people either blow through their first salary or become overly cautious and save it all. But here was someone who wanted to both enjoy life and plan for the future—a rare and admirable mindset.

I smiled and told him, "Kishore, your perspective is refreshing. The fact that you're asking these questions at the start of your career is impressive. It shows you're already ahead of the game. Let me share something with you: the *Li Ka-Shing Model*.

Li Ka-Shing, one of the richest people in Hong Kong, developed a financial strategy for young earners. The model divides income into five key categories to help people manage their money while living a fulfilling life. Let me break it down:

- **30% for living expenses**
- **20% for networking and building relationships**
- **15% for self-learning and skill development**

- **10% for traveling and recreation**

- **25% for investments**

But India isn't Hong Kong. Our culture, lifestyle, and priorities are very different. So, I've customized this model to better suit someone like you living in India. Here's the Indian version."

**The Customized Indian Financial Model for Kishore**

I pulled out my whiteboard and started jotting down numbers, breaking Kishore's ₹40,000 monthly income into four categories.

**1. Living Expenses (40%): ₹16,000**
"This is the most important part of your budget. ₹16,000 goes towards rent, groceries, transportation, electricity, and other essentials. You'll live comfortably without stretching your resources."

Kishore nodded thoughtfully. "₹16,000 sounds reasonable for my current needs. I think I can manage that."

**2. Networking and Socializing (15%): ₹6,000**
I explained, "Building connections is crucial,

especially in your line of work. Use this ₹6,000 to treat your colleagues to coffee, attend seminars, buy gifts for family, or celebrate small wins with friends. Investing in relationships can open doors you didn't even know existed."

Kishore smiled, "This is my favorite category so far. Treating colleagues might even get me out of a weekend sprint!"

We both laughed, and I added, "Exactly! Networking is about planting seeds that could grow into opportunities."

**3. Travel and Recreation (20%): ₹8,000**
"This category is for your happiness," I said. "Use this for weekend trips, hobbies, or recreational activities. Maybe it's a Goa trip, or maybe it's taking up a hobby like photography or gaming. The key is to recharge and enjoy life."

Kishore's face lit up, "So, I can plan that Group ooty trip guilt-free? Amazing!"

"Absolutely," I replied, "because you've already budgeted for it."

**4. Investments (25%): ₹10,000**
Now came the serious part. "Kishore, you're

young, and time is on your side. Investing ₹10,000 every month in equity mutual funds through a SIP can help you build substantial wealth over time."

He leaned forward, curious, "But how much will ₹10,000 a month actually grow into?"

I pulled up my calculator. "Let's say you increase your SIP by 5% every year as your salary grows. Over the next 15 years, with an expected annual return of 12%, your investments will grow to approximately **₹60,00,000**."

Kishore's jaw dropped. "Wait, what? ₹60lakhs just from investing ₹10,000 monthly? That's incredible!"

I grinned, "That's the power of compounding. Your money works for you and grows exponentially over time."

## A Practical Tip: Separate Bank Accounts for Better Management

To make Kishore's financial plan more effective and easy to follow, I introduced the concept of **dedicated bank accounts for different purposes**. This simple step would add a layer of discipline to his budgeting and make it effortless to track where his money was going.

Here's how I suggested Kishore set it up:

## 1. Account 1: Networking and Socializing

- **Purpose:** Use this account solely for networking-related expenses like treating colleagues to coffee, attending professional events, buying gifts for special occasions, or participating in team activities.

- **Why It Works:** By allocating a fixed amount each month (₹6,000 in Kishore's case), he wouldn't have to worry about overspending on social obligations. Even if he uses the entire balance, he knows it's within his budget.

- **Psychological Advantage:** Spending from this account creates a sense of freedom without guilt. Kishore could attend a team dinner or a friend's birthday celebration without second-guessing if he was cutting into funds meant for other priorities.

## 2. Account 2: Travel and Fun

- **Purpose:** This account would be dedicated to Kishore's recreation—short trips, hobbies, or indulging in experiences that bring him joy.

- **Why It Works:** Having a separate account ensures that travel and fun expenses don't get mixed up with essentials like rent or savings. It's easier to plan weekend getaways or enroll in a hobby class when the money is already set aside.

- **Psychological Advantage:** This separation allows Kishore to enjoy his ₹6,000 guilt-free, knowing it's specifically meant for enriching his life. He can say yes to spontaneous plans or even splurge occasionally, all while staying disciplined.

## 3. Salary Account: Living Expenses and Investments

- **Purpose:** Kishore could use his primary salary account for essential expenses like rent, groceries, and transportation (₹16,000) as well as for his investments (₹12,000).

- **Why It Works:** This account becomes the base for handling his fixed obligations and growing his wealth. It ensures that Kishore doesn't accidentally dip into his investment funds for non-essentials.

- **Psychological Advantage:** Watching his investment grow directly from this account would reinforce a sense of achievement and motivate him to save more.

## The Power of Separation

"By separating your money this way," I explained, "you're giving yourself *mental clarity and control.* Let me tell you why it works so well:

- You'll avoid the temptation to dip into your travel budget for random expenses.

- Networking and socializing won't feel like a financial burden since it's pre-planned.

- You won't overspend on one category and compromise your future goals."

This structure creates a system where every rupee is accounted for, yet Kishore would still feel free to enjoy his hard-earned salary.

## The Long-Term Perspective

I added, "As your salary increases, this setup will bring even more benefits. For example:

- Let's say your income rises to ₹60,000 in a two years. You'll allocate ₹24,000 for living right? But if you stick to the habit of living within ₹16,000–₹20,000, the remaining balance from your living expense allocation will automatically get saved.

- You'll feel happier because you'll still have more to spend on networking, travel, and investments as these percentages grow.

This framework not only helps you manage money today but also ensures you develop habits that make saving and spending easier as your income grows."

**In Summary:** Setting up separate accounts is not just a practical step—it's a mindset shift. It allows you to enjoy life, grow your wealth, and feel in control of your finances, all at the same time. For Kishore, this was the perfect way to turn confusion into confidence.

**The Psychological Aspect: Spending Wisely to Enjoy Fully**

I leaned back and said, "You know, Kishore, managing money isn't about being miserly or spending recklessly. It's about balance. By dividing your salary into these categories, you're giving every rupee a purpose.

- You'll feel secure knowing your living expenses are covered.

- You'll enjoy meaningful relationships by investing in networking.

- You'll experience the joys of life through travel and hobbies.

- And most importantly, you're building a future where money works for you, not the other way around.

When you live with intention, ₹40,000 will feel like ₹1,00,000. It's not just about the amount— it's about how you use it."

Kishore smiled, "This makes so much sense. I get to enjoy today without sacrificing my future.

This plan gives me both control and satisfaction."

**A Follow-Up: Progress in Action**

A month later, Sanjay called me, thrilled. "Kishore is following your advice perfectly. And here's the fun part—he's already opened separate accounts for networking and travel. He's even inspiring others in our office to plan their finances better."

I laughed, "Looks like Kishore is already becoming a financial role model!"

**Key Takeaways from Kishore's Journey**

1. **Structure Brings Clarity:** Dividing your income into categories ensures purposeful spending and saving.

2. **Discipline Pays Off:** Using separate accounts for different goals makes it easy to stick to the plan.

3. **Start Early, Reap Big:** Investing ₹10,000 monthly with incremental increases can lead to a corpus of ₹60 lakhs in 15 years.

4. **Celebrate Salary Hikes Wisely:** Habits of disciplined living allow you to save more when your income grows, creating a cycle of satisfaction and wealth.

5. **Enjoy Today, Plan for Tomorrow:** Striking a balance between present enjoyment and future security ensures a fulfilling financial journey.

With this simple yet effective plan, Kishore transformed confusion into clarity and set himself on a path to financial success and happiness.

# Case Study 11
## Ramesh's Twin Challenge: Two Kids, Two Weddings

One fine evening, as I was sipping my coffee and reflecting on the day's work, my phone buzzed. It was Ramesh, the familiar auto driver-turned-financial-planning-enthusiast from my previous case study. "Sir, can I meet you tomorrow? It's urgent!" he said, his voice carrying a hint of stress.

The next day, Ramesh arrived at my office, but this time, he wasn't alone. He brought his wife, Lakshmi, along. Both of them looked anxious, and I could sense this was something significant.

"Sir, we need your help," Ramesh began, almost hesitantly. "It's about our two kids."

I leaned forward and said, "Okay, tell me what's bothering you."

Ramesh continued, "Our daughter Meera is 15 years old, and Meghna is 15 as well—twins. In about 10 years, they'll be ready for marriage. We want to ensure we can give them both decent weddings, but with our current income and expenses, we're not sure how to plan for it. We don't want to compromise on their dreams, but we also don't want to fall into the trap of taking huge loans and drowning in debt."

Ah, the classic Indian parenting dilemma: aspirations vs. finances. I smiled and reassured them, "Ramesh, first of all, it's fantastic that you're thinking about this now. Many people wait until it's too late. But don't worry—we'll figure this out step by step."

**Breaking Down the Numbers: Budgeting for the Big Day**

I pulled out a piece of paper and asked, "What kind of budget are you thinking for each wedding?"

Ramesh and Lakshmi exchanged a look before Lakshmi spoke up. "Sir, we were thinking around ₹10,00,000 for each wedding. So, ₹20,00,000 for both. We think that should be enough for a simple wedding."

"Alright," I said, nodding. "But let's factor in inflation here. Weddings don't cost the same today as they did 10 years ago. Assuming an annual inflation rate of about 7%, ₹10,00,000 today will be approximately ₹20,00,000 in 10 years. So, for both weddings, we're looking at a total of ₹40,00,000."

Their jaws dropped. "₹40,00,000?!" Ramesh exclaimed.

"Yes," I nodded. "But don't worry. That's why we plan ahead."

**Setting Up a Plan**

"Ramesh," I continued, "I'm assuming you know a bit about how mutual funds work, right?"

He nodded enthusiastically. "Yes, sir! You explained it to me during our auto ride."

"Good! Here's what we'll do. You'll start a Systematic Investment Plan (SIP) specifically for the weddings. How much can you set aside each month?"

Ramesh and Lakshmi both looked at each other, a little unsure.

I turned to Lakshmi and asked, "How much can you contribute from your side? I mean, how much do you think you can save each month?"

She hesitated, then said, "Maybe ₹1,000 or ₹2,000."

It wasn't a shock to me. I understood that it's a common situation for many people nowadays.

"Okay," I said, "Do you track your expenses every month or create a budget?"

Lakshmi replied, "We used to do it when we were newly married, but after that, we kind of stopped."

I smiled and said, "No problem. Let's do that now."

## Budget Time: Understanding the Numbers

"Alright, don't worry. Let me create a budget for you," I said, taking out my pen and paper.

"Ramesh, tell me about your income."

Ramesh scratched his head and said, "As an auto driver, we don't have a fixed income. But if I had to estimate, it's around ₹55,000 a month."

"That's good," I said, encouraging him. "And what about your wife? Does she work or is she a housewife?"

"She works in a hospital canteen, and her salary is around ₹19,500."

I quickly did the math. "That brings your combined income to ₹74,500. That's not bad at all! You're doing quite well."

Both of them looked genuinely happy to hear that.

"Now, let's talk about your fixed expenses. What do you have in terms of regular payments, like rent or EMIs?"

Lakshmi quickly replied, "
Rent is **₹12,000** per month,
Ramesh's auto loan is **₹23,000**, and we bought a 55-inch TV and speaker on EMI last month, which is **₹7,500** per month for the next 12 months.
Both our daughters' tuition fees are **₹2,500** per

month, and the school fees are paid yearly, so that's not monthly." & SIP for new car **₹1,500** (Readers I hope you remember this **₹1,500 sip story if not please read case study 9)**

I listed them into my excel sheet

- **Rent**: ₹12,000
- **Auto Loan EMI**: ₹23,000
- **TV & Speaker EMI**: ₹7,500 (for the next 12 months)
- **Tuition Fees for Daughters**: ₹2,500 (monthly)
- **SIP for a New Car**: ₹1,500

"Alright," I said, writing it all down. "So, your total fixed expenses come to ₹46,500."

That left them with ₹28,000 for everything else.

"Now, let's allocate that remaining ₹28,000. For groceries, electricity, and gas bills, you'll need around ₹8,500. For entertainment and movies, set aside ₹4,000. It's going to feel tight for a while, but if you stick to this plan, whenever your salary increases, you can adjust it accordingly.

This should leave you with a balance of ₹15,500."

"That balance," I continued, "should go into mutual funds. But first, let's talk about how you plan for your kids' school fees. Those are one-time expenses every year, right?"

Lakshmi answered, "Yes, per kid, it's ₹18,500. So, for both, it's ₹37,000 annually."

"Okay," I said, "In the next 9 months, you'll need to arrange for this. Do you have a plan for that?"

She shook her head and said no.

"Alright," I said, "Here's my plan: You should invest ₹12,000 per month into equity mutual funds for the next 10 years. By increasing your SIP by ₹1,500 every year and assuming a 12% return, you'll accumulate about ₹38,00,000— close to your ₹40,00,000 target. Any small lumpsums, like a bonus or additional income, can help fill the small gap."

"But wait," I continued, "You still need to plan for your kids' annual school fees. So, for the next 9 months, invest the remaining ₹3,500 in liquid mutual funds. These are low-risk investments and won't fluctuate much. After 9 months, this will give you ₹31,500, though there will still be a deficit of ₹5,500. But hey, that's better than nothing! This way, you'll have 85% of the amount covered."

## The Retirement Plan: Building a Future for Tomorrow

"Now, here's one more thing," I said, turning to Ramesh. "How old are you?"

"44, sir," he replied.

"Alright," I said, "Here's another plan. Once your TV EMI is over, please stop buying things on EMI unless your income increases by 50%. Redirect the ₹7,500 EMI payment towards an equity mutual fund for your retirement.

Additionally, in 5 years, when your auto loan is fully repaid, redirect that ₹23,000 toward retirement as well. By doing this, and assuming a 12% annual return, you could accumulate approximately ₹70,00,000 by the time you're 60. Yes, it's a modest amount because of inflation, but it's a good start."

"But remember," I added, "This plan is based on your current situation. The future might bring surprises. Maybe Ramesh will start a business or Lakshmi could open her own canteen and earn much more. But for now, this plan is something we can stick to. It's better to have something than nothing!"

**Facing Concerns: Handling Setbacks and Uncertainties**

Lakshmi, who had been quiet till now, finally spoke up. "Sir, this sounds great, but what if we fall short even after this?"

"Lakshmi," I said, "planning is about preparation, not perfection. By starting today, you're already giving yourselves the best shot at achieving this dream. And remember, a wedding is not about how much money you spend but about the memories you create. Even if there's a small shortfall, it can be managed without stress because most of the heavy lifting will already be done through your SIPs."

Her face lit up at that, and she smiled. "That's true, sir. Thank you for explaining it so simply."

Ramesh and Lakshmi looked at each other, and I could see a sense of relief starting to wash over them. Ramesh smiled, his eyes a little brighter than before. "Sir, we didn't think we could ever plan for something like this. We were always so focused on surviving month by month."

I nodded. "That's how many people feel, but the key is to plan ahead. You don't need to make drastic changes overnight, but small, consistent efforts can make a big difference in the long run."

We spent some more time discussing their current financial habits, and I encouraged them to keep a close eye on their spending. "Remember," I told them, "the small things add up—tracking your expenses is just as important as investing."

Before they left, I gave them a final piece of advice. "As life evolves, so will your finances. Keep adjusting your SIPs, start saving more as your income increases, and always look for ways to reduce unnecessary expenses. By sticking to this plan, you'll be able to manage both your daughters' weddings and secure your future as well."

Ramesh thanked me with a warm handshake, and they left with more hope in their hearts than when they entered. I couldn't help but feel a sense of pride. Helping families like Ramesh and Lakshmi plan for the future, no matter how modest their income, was truly fulfilling.

And as I sat back in my chair, reflecting on the case once again, I realized that financial planning isn't just about numbers. It's about understanding a family's dreams, hopes, and aspirations—and helping them achieve those dreams one step at a time.

The plan we devised for Ramesh and Lakshmi wasn't perfect, and there might be bumps along the way. But it gave them the confidence to start, and that was all they needed to take the first step toward a secure financial future.

## Key Take aways

- **Early Planning is Key**: Ramesh and Lakshmi's proactive approach to planning for their children's weddings, even though they are still years away, is a great example of forward-thinking financial planning. Starting early ensures that financial goals can be achieved without stress or debt.
- **Balancing Aspirations and Finances**: While parents often want to provide the best for their children, it's essential to balance their aspirations with realistic financial planning. Ensuring that both

dreams and finances are aligned is critical to avoiding unnecessary strain.

- **Avoiding Debt for Life Events**: Ramesh's concern about taking on loans for their children's weddings highlights the importance of saving in advance. A well-thought-out savings plan can prevent falling into the trap of high-interest debt for such significant life events.

- **The Importance of Financial Guidance**: Ramesh reached out for professional financial suggestion. Consulting a financial planner early on helps families understand their financial situation better and make informed decisions regarding savings, investments, and budgeting for future goals.

- **The Power of Long-Term Vision**: Planning for major expenses like weddings, which might seem distant, requires setting long-term goals. Establishing a clear plan allows for smaller, manageable steps and avoids last-minute financial panic.

# CASE STUDY 12

## Creating a Retirement Corpus While Still Paying EMIs

It was Saturday evening, 5:30 PM. I was at my usual badminton game, looking forward to some much-needed relaxation after a busy week. At our court, we have eight players, so the games rotate. This means there's always a waiting period between matches.

As I waited for my turn, Arun, one of my court buddies, approached me and sat next to me. "Ganesh," he started hesitantly. "I've been meaning to talk to you about something important…"

I could sense the weight in his voice. "Sure, Arun! What's on your mind?" I asked, setting my racket aside.

"Well," he paused, looking a bit embarrassed, "it's about planning for my retirement. Meera and I are really confused. Can I come to your office to discuss it?"

"Of course, sir!" I said, immediately eager to help. "How about tomorrow morning at 9 AM?"

"But isn't tomorrow Sunday?" he asked, surprised.

"Yes, but I keep my Sundays flexible," I replied with a grin. "Just make sure we wrap up by 10:30 AM, or my wife might send some bouncers to bring me home!"

Arun burst out laughing. "Okay, okay, I promise I won't take more than 1.5 hours," he assured me.

## Sunday Morning: Diving In

The next morning, Arun and Meera arrived at my office sharp at 9 AM. I greeted them warmly. "Good morning! Coffee or tea?" I asked as they settled in.

"Coffee, please," they said in unison. As we sipped our drinks, I got straight to the point. "So, Arun and Meera, what's the situation?" I asked gently.

Arun sighed. "Honestly, Ganesh, it feels like we're stuck. We're both 42 years old now, and retirement is something we've been meaning to plan for years, but life just keeps getting in the way. But our EMIs are eating up most of our income. Every time we think about saving for the future, our loans seem to mock us."

Meera nodded, adding, "We've tried reading articles and watching videos on retirement planning, but the information is overwhelming. It feels like we're already behind, and that makes us anxious."

"Don't worry. You've already taken the first step by coming here. Let's take it step by step. First, I'll need a clear picture of your current financial situation. Numbers always tell the truth, so let's lay everything out," I said.

**Current Financial Picture**

After a brief discussion, Arun and Meera shared their financial details:

**Income:**

- Arun's monthly income: ₹1,25,000

- Meera's monthly income: ₹35,000
- **Total Monthly Income:** ₹1,60,000

**EMIs:**

- Housing Loan: ₹72,000 (20 years remaining)
- Car Loan: ₹18,000 (2 years remaining)
- Personal Loan: ₹10,000 (1 year remaining)
- **Total Monthly EMIs:** ₹1,00,000

**Savings/Investments:**

- Fixed Deposit (Emergency Fund): ₹3,50,000
- Stocks: ₹2,00,000
- PPF: ₹24,00,000 (5 years remaining; planned for son's higher education, expected to grow to ₹41,00,000 at 7.5% annual returns).

## Defining the Retirement Goal

I leaned back and asked, "If you were to retire today, how much money would you need each month to maintain your current lifestyle?"

They thought for a moment before Arun replied, "₹45,000 per month should cover all our expenses."

"Great," I said. "Now let's factor in inflation. Assuming you both plan to retire at 60, that gives us 18 years. At an inflation rate of 6%, ₹45,000 today will be equivalent to approximately ₹1,28,000 per month when you retire.

To sustain this for 30 years post-retirement, adjusting for inflation and assuming a 7%

withdrawal rate, you'll need a corpus of approximately ₹3.5 crores."

Their jaws dropped in unison. "₹3.5 crores?!" Arun exclaimed.

"Yes," I said. "But don't worry; we'll work out a step-by-step plan to get there.

## Breaking Down the Numbers

"Remember, this ₹3.5 crore figure includes inflation-adjusted withdrawals. For example, in your first year of retirement, you'll need ₹1,28,000 per month. In the second year, factoring in 5% inflation, your monthly need will rise by ₹6,500 to ₹1,35,500. The year after, it will increase by another ₹6,500, and so on. Inflation doesn't retire just because you do!"

They nodded, finally beginning to grasp the numbers.

## An Interesting Twist to the Numbers

I paused for a moment and added, "Here's something even more fascinating, Arun. Despite increasing withdrawals to keep up with inflation, after 30 years of retirement, your corpus will still have a balance of ₹4,12,84,000!

"How's that possible?" Arun asked, intrigued.

"It's simple," I explained. "Let's assume you invest this in a conservative category mutual fund. In the first year, you'll withdraw ₹15,36,000 (₹1,28,000 × 12). That's just 4.3% of your corpus. But here's the magic: your invested mutual fund has the potential to generate around 7% returns annually.

"Even as you increase your withdrawals each year to keep up with inflation, your corpus continues to grow. For example, in the second year, you'll withdraw ₹16,26,000 (₹1,35,500 × 12), which is ₹90,000 more than the first year. This pattern of inflation-adjusted increases will continue year after year, yet your investments will still generate enough returns to offset these rising withdrawals.

"The portion you don't withdraw will keep compounding with the existing corpus, allowing your investments to not only sustain your lifestyle but also grow significantly. Over time, this growth outpaces the impact of inflation and withdrawals, leaving you with a healthy balance even after 30 years."

**The Action Plan : The Roadmap to ₹3.5 Crores**

"Now," I said, "you both have ₹60,000 left after paying your EMIs. Here's what we'll do:

1. **Year 1:**

   o Live within ₹38,000 per month for household expenses.

   o Invest the remaining ₹22,000 as a SIP in equity mutual funds. Increase this SIP by ₹2,500 every year.

2. **Year 2:**

   o Your personal loan of ₹10,000 will be paid off. Redirect that amount to SIPs, making it ₹32,000 per month (22,000 +10,000). Add the ₹2,500 increment, and you'll be investing ₹34,500 monthly.

3. **Year 3:**

   o Your car loan of ₹18,000 will also be paid off. Redirect that amount too, taking your SIPs to ₹52,500

(34500+18000) per month. Add the annual increment of ₹2,500, making it ₹55,000.

4. **For the Next 16 Years:**

   ○ Continue SIPs at ₹55,000 per month, increasing by ₹2,500 every year. At an assumed return of 12% per annum, this will grow to ₹4 crores by the time you turn 60.

## Addressing Parallel Goals

I turned to Meera and said, "For your son's higher education, your PPF investments are perfectly aligned. With ₹24,00,000 already invested, it will grow to ₹41,00,000 in five years. This will cover all your planned expenses for his education. So, you're already ahead on that front."

Both Arun and Meera smiled, visibly relieved.

## Practical Insights and Encouragement

"Arun, Meera," I concluded, "retirement planning isn't about luxury; it's about security. By starting today and sticking to the plan, you're not just

building a future for yourselves—you're also
setting a financial example for your son.

"And remember, it's okay to start small. The key
is consistency. SIPs are like planting a tree; they
grow slowly at first, but with time, they give you
shade and fruits."

Meera said, "This makes so much sense now.
Thank you, Ganesh. We finally feel like we're in
control."

As they left my office, I couldn't help but feel a deep sense of satisfaction. Helping families like Arun and Meera is the reason I love what I do.

## Moral of the Story

Planning for retirement might seem overwhelming, but it's all about breaking it into manageable steps. With discipline, patience, and expert guidance, anyone can secure their financial future.

## Key Take Aways

- **Start Planning Early**: Taking the first step in retirement planning, even if it seems overwhelming, is essential. The sooner you start, the better prepared you'll be.
- **Assess Your Financial Situation**: A clear understanding of your current income, expenses, loans, and investments is crucial in building a successful retirement plan.

- **Account for Inflation**: Inflation will increase your future expenses, so it's important to adjust your retirement goals to account for it.
- **Benefit from Compound Growth**: Even after withdrawals, a well-invested portfolio can grow through the power of compounding, helping to sustain your retirement corpus.
- **Create a Step-by-Step Plan**: A structured and consistent approach to saving and investing is key to reaching your retirement goal.
- **Discipline and Consistency Are Crucial**: Small, regular investments over time often lead to greater success than larger, one-time contributions.
- **Peace of Mind Through Planning**: A clear, actionable plan can reduce anxiety and give you control over your financial future.
- **Patience Pays Off**: Retirement planning is a long-term endeavor, and success comes with patience, consistency, and the right guidance.

# Case Study 13
## Mr. Rao's Quest: Higher Returns with Principal Safety

It was a peaceful Sunday afternoon, and Mr. Rao, a 65-year-old retiree, was sitting comfortably in his living room, sipping tea and flipping through the pages of his favorite newspaper. As he read the stock market updates, his mind wandered to the future—specifically, his grandson, Arjun. He had always been close to him, and now that Arjun was growing up, Mr. Rao had an idea. He wanted to make sure that Arjun would have a strong financial foundation when he turned 18, so he could use the money for his higher education or even start his own venture.

Mr. Rao wasn't the type to take unnecessary risks with his savings. Being from a generation that valued stability, he'd always kept his money in Fixed Deposits (FDs). After all, they were safe, right? But as he glanced at the interest rates on FDs, which had been steadily decreasing, he couldn't help but feel that his money could work harder for him—without compromising safety.

With a sigh, he set the newspaper down and called his financial planner, none other than me. We've had a good relationship for the last four years. "Ganesh, I need your suggestion. I've ₹5,00,000 in my savings account, and I want to invest it in a way that will grow but also keep my principal safe. I want to give this money as a gift to my grandson when he turns 18 which is 10 years from now. But I need it to grow faster than the interest I'd get from an FD. What can I do?"

I said, "Hmm, that's a bit challenging because the returns are directly proportional to the risk that you're taking. So, if you want returns higher than FD, you'll have to take on some risk."

Mr. Rao said, "Yes, Ganesh, I can understand that, but in any case, I should not lose my principal—that's my main concern. Are there no options available?"

I thought for a while, then I got an idea.

"I have just the right approach for you, Mr. Rao. It's called the Profit Transfer Concept, and I think it's perfect for your needs."

Mr. Rao leaned in, intrigued. "Profit Transfer? What's that? Sounds like something out of a fancy finance book!"

I said, "I'm suggesting you invest ₹5,00,000 in a Liquid Mutual Fund and transfer the profits generated from that investment into an Equity Mutual Fund—on a monthly basis."

Mr. Rao's voice shot up in surprise. "Transfer profits? Monthly? I've never heard of that before. Tell me more!"

## The Concept of Profit Transfer: A Safe Start with Growth Potential

I took a deep breath and began explaining. "Alright, Mr. Rao, let's break this down. A Liquid Fund is one of the safest mutual fund categories, typically investing in short-term debt instruments like treasury bills, which have a very low risk. This ensures that your principal of ₹5,00,000 is safe. However, the returns from a Liquid Fund, while relatively stable, tend to be lower than what you would get from riskier investments like equity funds."

"Okay, that sounds reasonable," he said, nodding thoughtfully.

" Now, here's the magic. Instead of keeping your interest or profits in the Liquid Fund, you transfer them every month into an Equity Mutual Fund— specifically into a Midcap Fund. Let me explain it with an example: Suppose you invest ₹5,00,000 this month. Next month, if the value grows to ₹5,03,000, the additional ₹3,000 will be transferred to the Equity Mutual Fund. This strategy allows your money to grow at a faster pace because mid-cap stocks tend to give higher returns than large-cap stocks over the long term. The key here is that your principal stays safely in the Liquid Fund, but the profits from that fund are working hard in the equity market, giving you the best of both worlds—security and growth!"

Mr. Rao seemed intrigued but still a little skeptical. "But how do we know this will actually work? You know, over time?"

I smiled and said, "Well, let me show you an example with real historical data."

## The Historical Example: ICICI Liquid Fund to ICICI Pru Midcap Fund (2014-2024)

"Let's take a look at what would have happened if you had followed this strategy over the past decade," I said, opening my laptop to take data.

Let's assume you had invested ₹5,00,000 in December 2014 into the ICICI Liquid Fund, and we would have transferred the profits from that investment into the ICICI Prudential Midcap Fund. Over the past ten years, you would have transferred ₹3,10,400 as profit from ICICI Liquid Fund to ICICI Midcap Fund in total, which is a 6.49% average return on the liquid fund.

I continued, "The ICICI Pru Midcap Fund, the fund that gets transfers from the liquid mutual fund, over the last decade, generated an average annual return of 18.58%. So, the ₹3,10,400 transferred over the years have grown to ₹8,75,000."

Mr. Rao said, "Wait a minute. So, you're telling me that after 10 years, I would have ₹8,75,000 in equity funds from just the profits, plus the ₹5,00,000 that remained in the Liquid Fund? That means ₹13,75,000 in total?"

"Exactly," I said. "Your total corpus would be ₹13,75,000—₹5,00,000 in the Liquid Fund and ₹8,75,000 in the Equity Fund. The combined average return comes to 10.57%, which is greater than FD returns, as you asked. And all this comes from a strategy where your principal was safe, but your profits were working hard in the equity market."

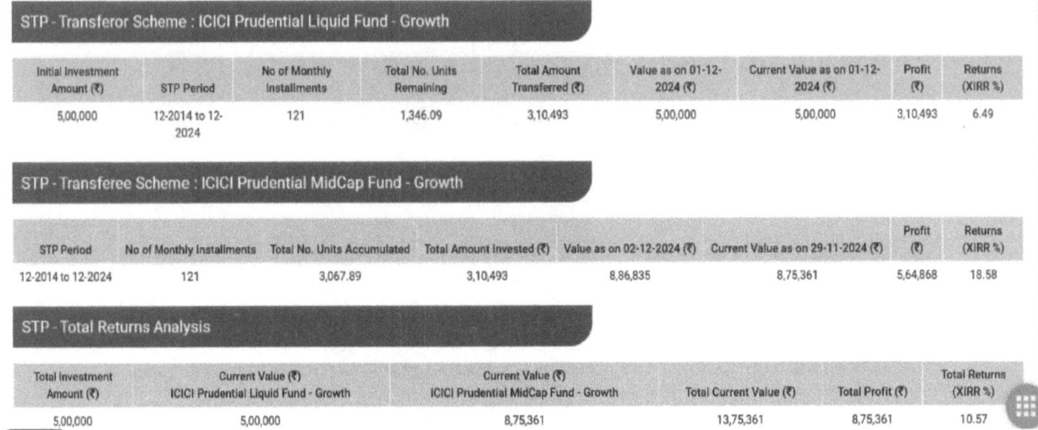

**STP - Transferor Scheme : ICICI Prudential Liquid Fund - Growth**

| Initial Investment Amount (₹) | STP Period | No of Monthly Installments | Total No. Units Remaining | Total Amount Transferred (₹) | Value as on 01-12-2024 (₹) | Current Value as on 01-12-2024 (₹) | Profit (₹) | Returns (XIRR %) |
|---|---|---|---|---|---|---|---|---|
| 5,00,000 | 12-2014 to 12-2024 | 121 | 1,346.09 | 3,10,493 | 5,00,000 | 5,00,000 | 3,10,493 | 6.49 |

**STP - Transferee Scheme : ICICI Prudential MidCap Fund - Growth**

| STP Period | No of Monthly Installments | Total No. Units Accumulated | Total Amount Invested (₹) | Value as on 02-12-2024 (₹) | Current Value as on 29-11-2024 (₹) | Profit (₹) | Returns (XIRR %) |
|---|---|---|---|---|---|---|---|
| 12-2014 to 12-2024 | 121 | 3,067.89 | 3,10,493 | 8,86,835 | 8,75,361 | 5,64,868 | 18.58 |

**STP - Total Returns Analysis**

| Total Investment Amount (₹) | Current Value (₹) ICICI Prudential Liquid Fund - Growth | Current Value (₹) ICICI Prudential MidCap Fund - Growth | Total Current Value (₹) | Total Profit (₹) | Total Returns (XIRR %) |
|---|---|---|---|---|---|
| 5,00,000 | 5,00,000 | 8,75,361 | 13,75,361 | 8,75,361 | 10.57 |

## What About Future Expectations?

Mr. Rao asked, "That sounds fantastic! But how realistic is this for the future?"

"Great question, Mr. Rao," I said. "Since we can't predict future returns exactly, let's make a reasonable assumption. Over the next 10 years, you can assume this strategy may give a return of 9%."

"If we apply these numbers," I continued, "your ₹5,00,000 may grow to ₹11,80,000 by applying this strategy."

Mr. Rao looked pleased, but I could sense that he was still processing the numbers. "So, you're saying that this strategy could actually grow my

₹5,00,000 gift to ₹11,80,000? With the principal safe?"

"Yes, Mr. Rao. The key here is the power of consistent compounding, where the growth from both the Liquid Fund and the Midcap Fund works together. And most importantly, your principal remains safe in the Liquid Fund. This strategy not only outperforms FD returns but gives you the growth you need to leave a significant gift for your grandson."

## The Gift for the Grandson

Mr. Rao replied with a smile spreading across his face. "You know, Ganesh, I've always wanted to leave something substantial for my grandson, but I didn't know how. This plan sounds like the perfect solution. I'm happy to know that not only will the ₹5,00,000 be secure, but it will also grow significantly over the next 10 years."

"Exactly," I replied. "This strategy not only secures the present but also builds wealth for the future. By transferring just the profits, you're maximizing your returns while keeping your principal untouched."

Mr. Rao said, "Thank you, Ganesh. I feel much more confident now. I can already picture my grandson opening that gift when he turns 18."

**Key Takeaways from Mr. Rao's Story:**

1. **Profit Transfer:** The concept of transferring profits from a liquid fund to an equity fund each month allows for growth without risking the principal.

2. **Long-Term Growth Potential:** Over time, the profits accumulated from liquid funds and transferred into equity funds can significantly grow, leading to a much larger corpus.

3. **Minimized Risk, Maximized Return:** Since only profits are being transferred, the risk is minimized while still benefiting from the higher returns of equity funds.

4. **Compound Growth:** By regularly transferring profits to an equity fund, the returns on those profits compound over time, significantly boosting the final amount.

5. **A Great Strategy for Long-Term Goals:** This strategy works well for long-term goals like gifting a lump sum to a loved one, as it balances safety with growth.

By following this approach, Mr. Rao was able to create a meaningful and substantial gift for his grandson, showing that with a little strategy, even conservative investors can achieve impressive growth without compromising on safety.

# Case Study 14

## Rekha's Journey: Diversifying 100% Real Estate Assets for a Better Future

Life doesn't always follow the script we imagine for it. Rekha, a strong, determined woman in her mid-40s, knows this better than most. Five years ago, her life turned upside down when her husband, her partner and support system, passed away suddenly. Left with three houses, a teenage son, and a mountain of responsibility, Rekha had no time to wallow in grief. Her new life demanded all her strength, and she poured herself into managing her family's only source of income—rental properties.

"I've done everything I can to make sure my son and I are secure," she said, sitting across from me, her eyes both tired and determined. "But I'm starting to wonder—am I really using what I have in the best possible way? What if something goes wrong? What if this isn't enough?"

Rekha's question hit a deep chord. As a financial planner, I've seen this fear in so many people—the worry that their efforts, no matter how sincere, might not be enough to secure the future. But I've also seen something else: the immense potential of thoughtful planning and the courage to make bold, transformative decisions.

**Rekha's Current Situation**

Rekha's financial reality was straightforward but deeply unbalanced. She owned three houses:

1. **House 1:** A ₹1,00,00,000 property in a prime area of Chennai, earning a monthly rent of ₹35,000.

2. **House 2:** A ₹1,85,00,000 property in another central location, earning ₹45,000 monthly.

3. **House 3:** An ₹85,00,000 property on the outskirts of Chennai, earning just ₹15,000 monthly.

Her total rental income was ₹95,000 per month—a respectable amount, but it came with limitations. When Rekha calculated the rental yield (annual rent as a percentage of property value), she found it was just 3% across the board.

"Three percent," she said, shaking her head. "That's much lower than my savings bank interest. But I've always thought real estate was the safest place for money."

"That's a common belief," I replied. "And it's not wrong—real estate can be a great investment. But putting 100% of your wealth into one asset class is like walking a tightrope without a safety net. What happens if there's a slowdown in the property market, or if tenants move out?"

She sighed, visibly frustrated. "I've been so focused on managing these properties that I never thought about alternatives. But I don't want to live with this stress forever. I want stability, and more than that, I want to know my son will have a secure future."

**Exploring New Perspectives on Wealth**

Before diving into numbers, I shared a simple yet powerful philosophy with Rekha: **"Money is a tool, not a trophy."**

"Rekha," I began, "real wealth isn't about owning more or holding on to what feels safe. It's about using what you have to create the life you want. Your properties are incredible tools—but tools need to be sharpened, updated, and sometimes even swapped out to do their best work."

**Unlocking the Potential of the Third House**

We started by focusing on House 3, the property on the outskirts of Chennai. Rekha's husband purchased it five years ago for ₹65,00,000, and it had appreciated to ₹85,00,000—a decent gain, but its rental income was the lowest of her three properties.

"Rekha, this house isn't pulling its weight," I explained. "Outer-city properties often appreciate more slowly than urban ones, and they tend to have lower rental demand. If you sell this house, you can use the proceeds to create a diversified portfolio that generates both stable income and long-term growth."

She hesitated. "Selling feels so final. What about the capital gains tax? Won't that eat into the money?"

"That's a valid concern," I said, pulling up a calculator. "Under the new tax rules, your capital gain of ₹20,00,000 will be taxed at 12.5% since indexation benefits don't apply anymore. That's ₹2,50,000 in tax, leaving you with ₹82,50,000. But think about this: you bought the house for ₹65,00,000. Even after tax, you've grown your investment significantly. Now, let's put that ₹82,50,000 to work."

**Building a Diversified Portfolio**

## 1. Fixed Deposits for Stability (30% Allocation)

"Let's start with safety," I said. "We'll put ₹24,75,000 into fixed deposits. At an interest rate of 7%, this will give you ₹14,000 per month—a predictable income stream you can rely on."

## 2. Mutual Funds for Growth (70% Allocation)

Next, we allocated the remaining ₹57,75,000 across carefully selected mutual funds:

- **Balanced Advantage Fund (30%):** ₹17,32,500

  "This fund dynamically shifts between equity and debt, giving you growth with less risk."

- **Conservative Hybrid Fund (30%):** ₹17,32,500

  "This is a great middle-ground investment. It prioritizes safety but offers better returns than fixed deposits."

- **Aggressive Hybrid Fund (20%):** ₹11,55,000

  "With a higher equity component, this fund is designed for long-term wealth creation."

- **Nifty Index Fund (20%):** ₹11,55,000
  "Index funds are simple, giving you exposure to the top-performing companies in the market."

## 3. Withdrawal Strategy

"From this mutual fund portfolio, you can withdraw 6% annually, which works out to ₹28,000 per month. To keep up with inflation, you can increase this withdrawal by ₹1,500 each year, just like you increase your rent annually."

Adding these new income streams to her existing rental income of first two houses, ₹80,000 , Rekha's total monthly income now reached **₹1,22,000**—a solid **₹27,000 additional income** from her earlier total.

Her face lit up with relief. "Wow! That's more than I ever thought I could get without taking on extra tenants or properties. It's like giving myself a raise!"

## The Philosophy of Compounding

But Rekha was curious about how this plan would play out in the long run. "What happens to my corpus as I withdraw from it? Won't it get depleted?"

"Great question," I replied. "Rekha, even as you withdraw 6% annually, your suggested mutual fund investments are expected to grow at an average rate of 9%. This means your withdrawals are covered by the returns, and the remaining growth keeps compounding. Over 15 years, your ₹57,75,000 corpus will grow to approximately ₹76,70,000, even after all the withdrawals."

Her eyes widened. "So my money grows even as I use it? That feels… almost great."

I replied with a smile. "It's the power of compounding, and it's available to anyone who invests wisely."

**A New Chapter for Rekha**

As we wrapped up our discussion, Rekha looked visibly relieved. "I came here feeling stuck, but now I see possibilities I never imagined. This plan gives me security, flexibility, and the confidence that my son and I will be okay."

"Rekha," I said, "this isn't just about numbers. It's about changing the way you see your wealth. You're no longer just a landlord; you're an investor, a planner, and someone who's actively shaping her future. That's powerful."

**Key takeaways:  Lessons from Rekha's Journey**

1. **Wealth Is a Journey, Not a Destination:** Real wealth isn't about hoarding assets— it's about using them to create the life you envision.

2. **Diversification Brings Stability:** Spreading investments across different asset classes reduces risk and unlocks growth opportunities.

3. **Compounding Is Your Best Friend:** Reinvesting returns creates exponential growth, even while you withdraw funds.

4. **Mindset Matters:** Letting go of "safe" but unproductive investments can open the door to greater possibilities.

5.  **A Plan Is Empowering:** With the right
    strategy, even life's uncertainties feel more
    manageable.

## Conclusion: Rekha's Bright Future

As Rekha left my office that day, she carried not just a financial plan but a renewed sense of purpose. She knew that her husband's legacy—the houses they built together—was no longer just a lifeline. With thoughtful planning and diversification, it had become a foundation for her and her son's brighter, more secure future.

In Rekha's story, we see the power of planning, the importance of mindset, and the incredible potential of money when it's treated as a tool for growth rather than a mere safety net.

## Congratulations, You've Reached the Finish Line!

As you turn the final page of this book, I hope you find yourself empowered with new insights, perspectives, and tools to navigate the world of personal finance. Whether you're just beginning your journey or already well on your way, remember that every decision you make today shapes the future you'll experience tomorrow.

Financial freedom isn't a destination; it's a journey that requires patience, discipline, and a bit of risk-taking. But most importantly, it requires belief in yourself and your ability to take control of your financial destiny.

I've shared with you stories, case studies, and ideas that are inspired by my experiences and the people I've worked with. **However, these are not 100% real events**. I've added some 'masala and pepper' to make them more engaging and relatable. While the core lessons remain practical and actionable, these stories are meant to illustrate key financial concepts rather than depict actual events. It's up to you to take these insights, apply them, and transform your future.

Thank you for allowing me to be a part of your journey. The road ahead may not always be smooth, but with the right mindset, a clear plan, and the courage to act, I have no doubt that you can build a future filled with financial security and lasting success.

I'm excited to see where this knowledge takes you. The next chapter of your life is just beginning—and I'm cheering for you every step of the way.

Until next time,
**Vishal Muralidharan, CFP, CRA**

If you'd like to connect or have any questions, feel free to reach out to me at:
**WhatsApp: 9789970712**